Daylight

ENCOUNTERS
TBow Bowden

Portraits of Americans

Cofounders: Taj Forer and Michael Itkoff
Creative Director: Ursula Damm
Copy Editor: Gabrielle Fastman

© 2022 Daylight Community Arts Foundation

Photographs © 2022 by Tom "TBow" Bowden / T. Bowden Productions, Inc.

"Inside the Head of Tom 'TBow' Bowden" © 2022 Tom "TBow" Bowden
"Shooting from the Heart" © 2022 by Maggie Steber

ISBN: 978-1-954119-18-5

Printed by Ofset Yapimevi, Turkey

Daylight Books
E-mail: info@daylightbooks.org
Web: www.daylightbooks.org

"IF YOU LOOK
THROUGH THE LENS
LONG ENOUGH AND
HARD ENOUGH,
WONDERFUL THINGS
WILL APPEAR."

—TBow

SHOOTING FROM THE HEART

by Maggie Steber

I first met TBow several years ago in Miami. Over a period of time, I saw and learned so much about the street and about TBow through his photographs. As much as they are stories about others, they are also about the person who made them.

The streets are constant theater and everyone on them is an actor of sorts. The people TBow finds and photographs remind me of Shakespearean characters. Sometimes I think they find him, as if there were a magnet between photographer and subject. They are drawn to each other. What is more astounding is TBow's connection to the people he photographs. He cares about them, is truly interested, not just for the sake of a photo, but because he wants to hear their stories.

The photographs are intimate and sardonic; some are heartbreaking and others are valiant. When their stories are included, the photographs become real to us. The portraits jump off the page. TBow finds a power in people that is hypnotic and intoxicating. If there is sometimes a certain despondency or loneliness displayed in some of his images, there is also an abundance of resilience, pride, and strength.

TBow's interest is genuine and respectful. He makes friends, and when you read what he has written about himself you understand that these people and the act of photographing them is his oxygen, his reason to get up every day to be on the streets with the heroes of his photographs. He is joyful in what he does. He is not a hit-and-run photographer. He is recording life.

Many of the photographs remind me of the work done by photographer Diane Arbus, who was also attracted to the street and people with some kind of character. I'm also reminded of the great Jill Freedman, who photographed life on the streets of New York like nobody else, as well as Robert Frank, whose photographs held up a mirror to show us who we really are as a nation.

Nowadays, much of street photography is detached. Not TBow's. He is a visual minstrel and troubadour. People are comfortable with him and they reveal their stories. Take Kat and Freddie, train hoppers who renewed their marital vows in New Orleans each year, until Freddie's drunken rage ended it all. Or Chris, a gentleman who goes by his Tibetan name, Chotak, and writes poems about his loneliness. There is also

Stephen, a homeless man whose daughter gave him her Hello Kitty backpack after she went to live with her mom.

TBow's photographs are stunning in their power to hold our attention and tug at our hearts and our minds, stopping us in our tracks and helping us appreciate these people whom we might have passed on the street without a second thought.

TBow writes himself reminders of what he seeks. Photography is his therapy. Here he can break the rules. He sees beyond the obvious, reminds himself to ask what happened. He questions why we are here together. The streets are where he finds life and love and loss and courage and eccentricity, and images that are like gifts waiting to be opened. He takes those gifts and shares them with us and we are made the wiser and better for seeing them.

Maggie Steber is a documentary photographer whose work focuses on humanitarian, cultural, and social stories. She has received numerous honors, including the Leica Medal of Excellence, and her work has appeared in publications such as National Geographic, Newsweek, *the* New York Times Magazine, *and the* Guardian. *Her monograph,* Dancing on Fire: Photographs from Haiti, *was published by Aperture.*

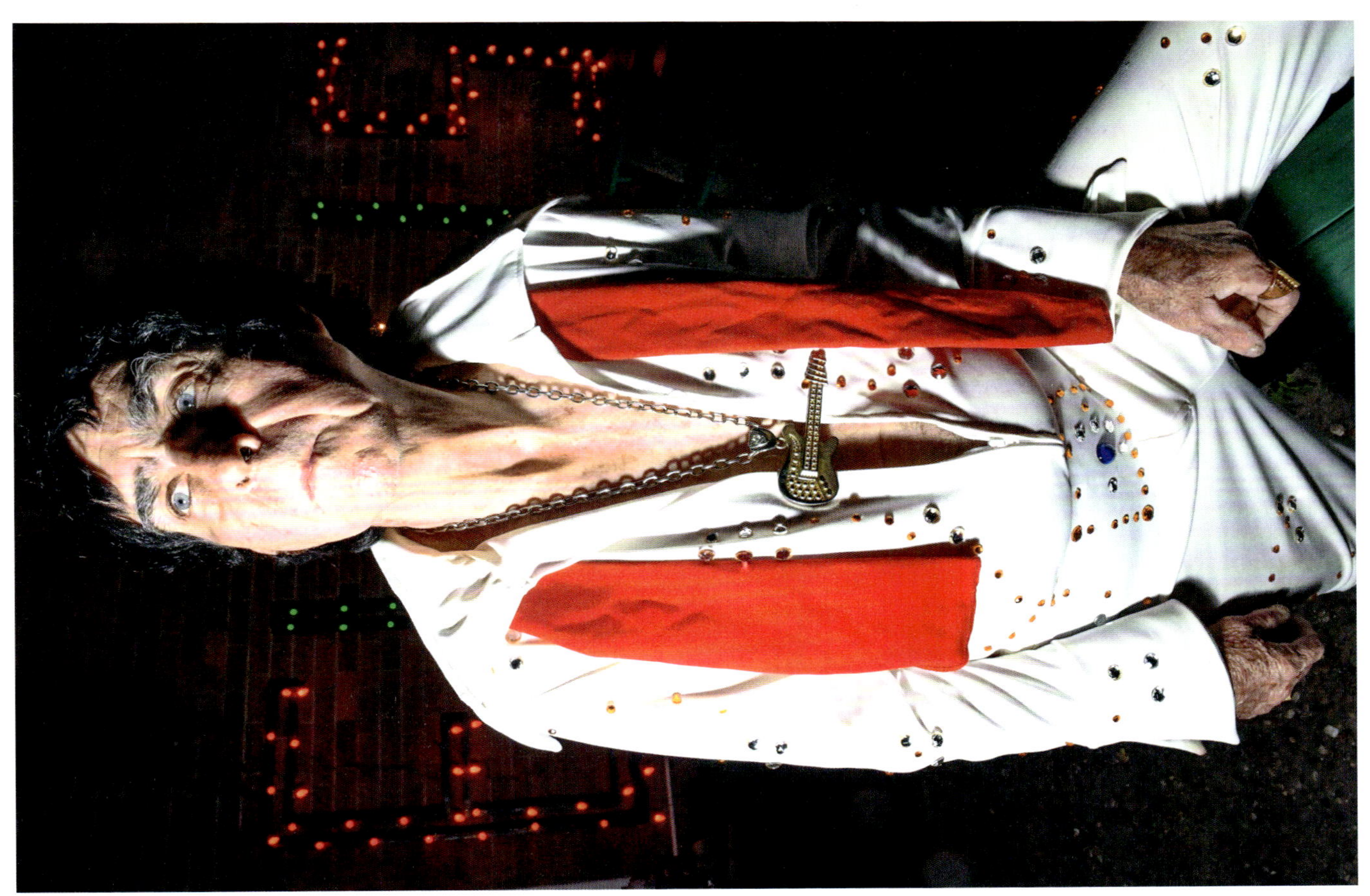

Elvis, Houston, Texas, 2018

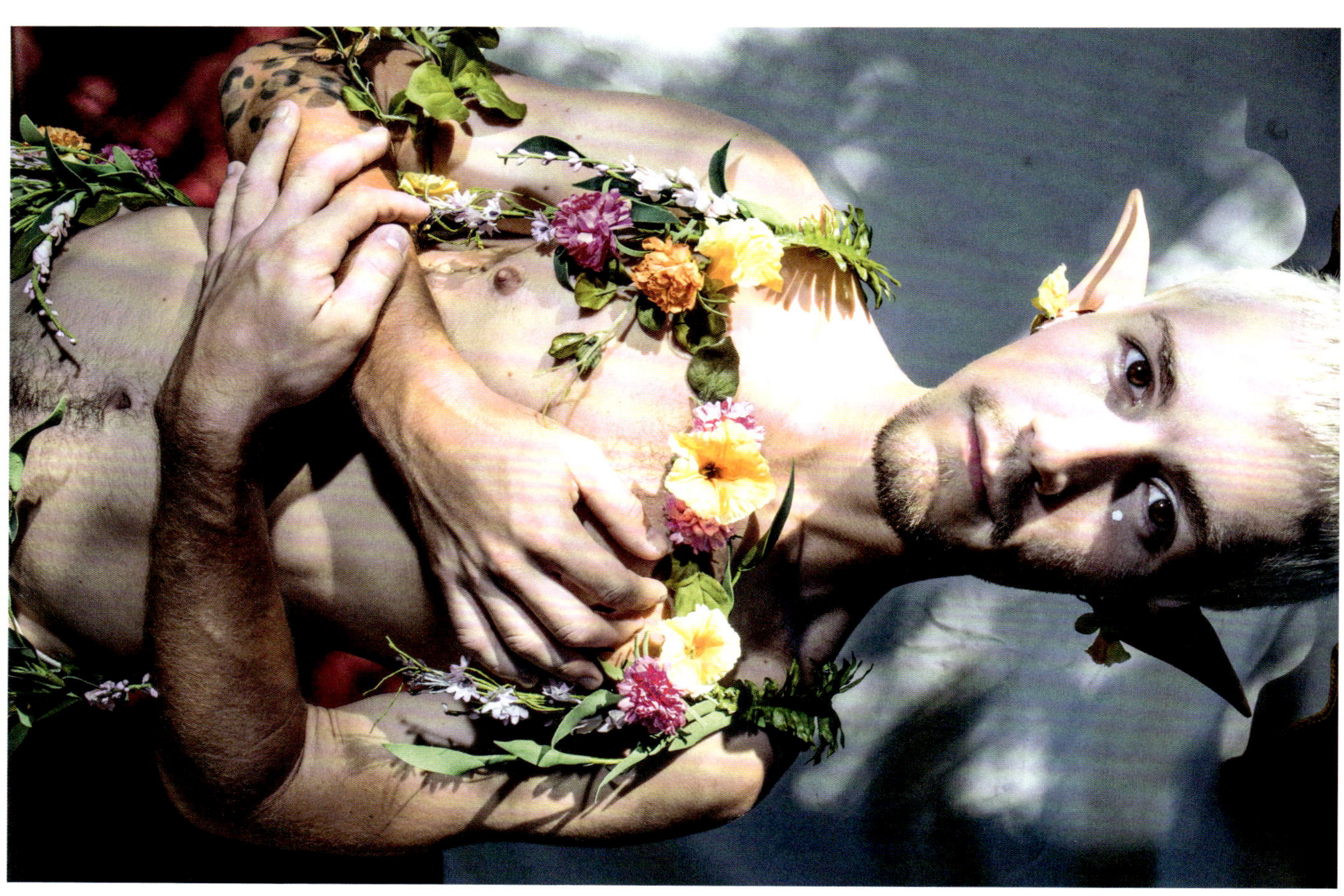

Flower Child, Todd Mission, Texas, 2016

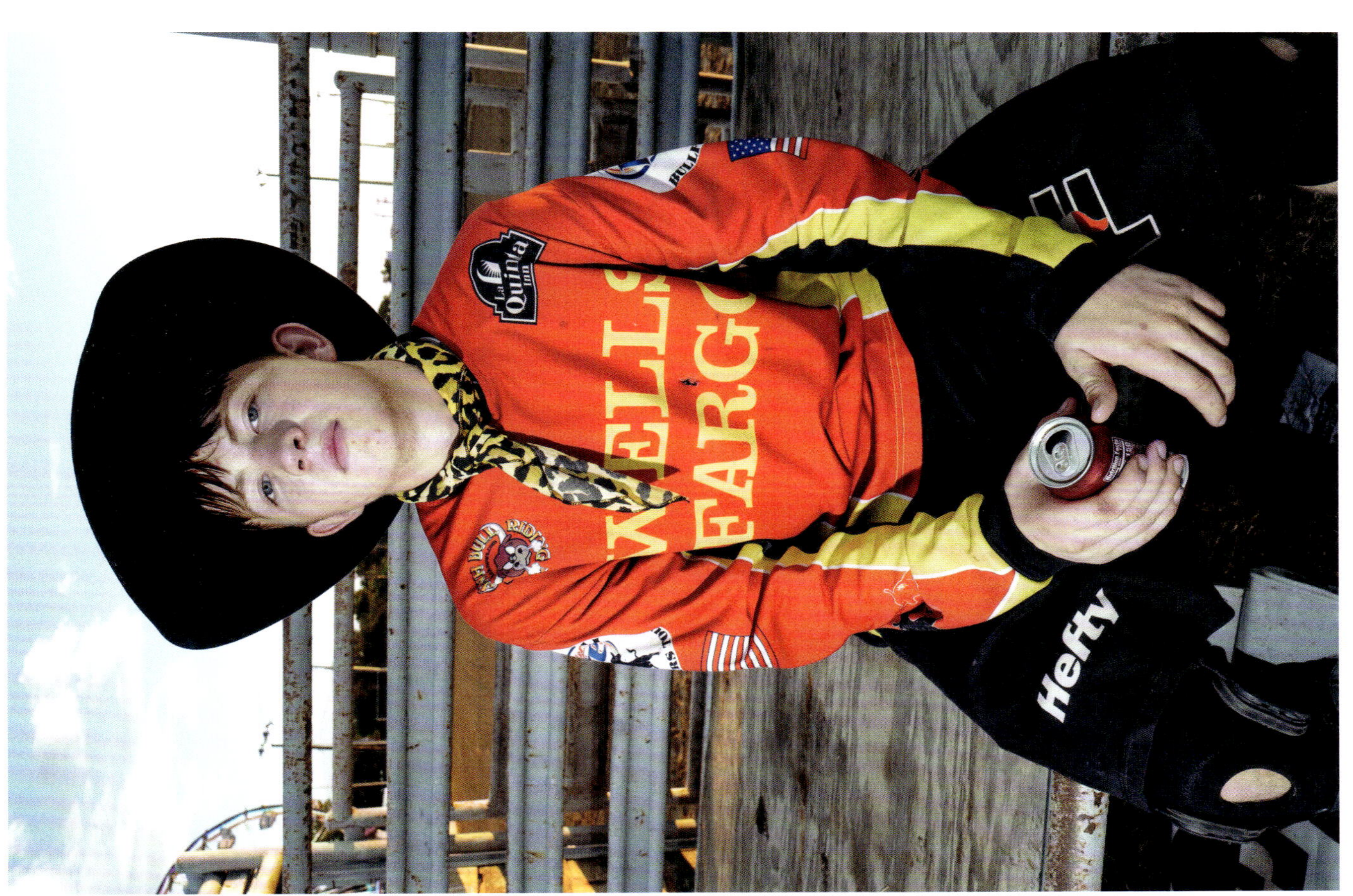

Dylan, Bullfighter, Brenham, Texas, 2021

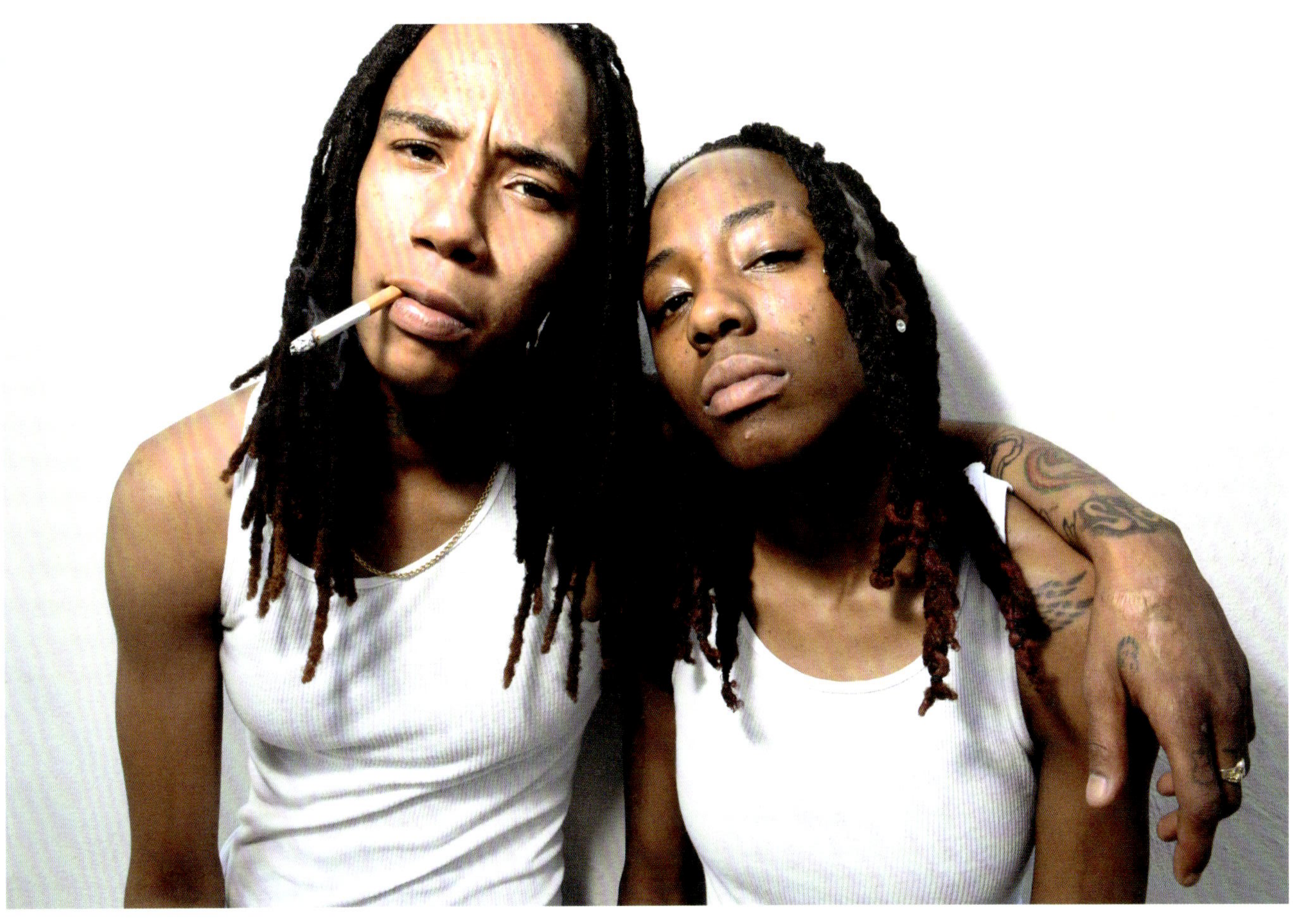

Jazz and Lokey, Miami, Florida, 2017

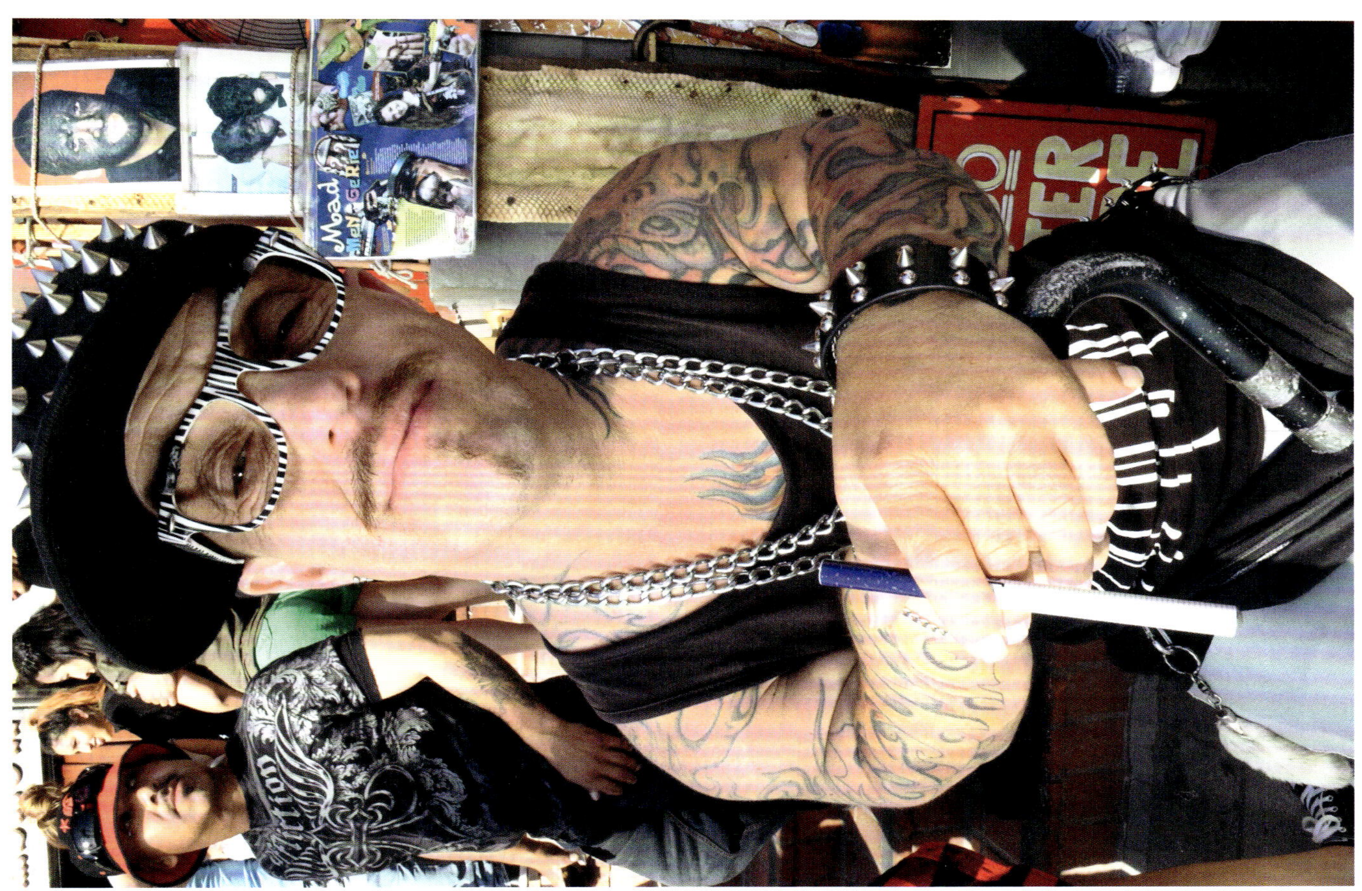

Carnival Hawker, Venice Beach, California, 2017

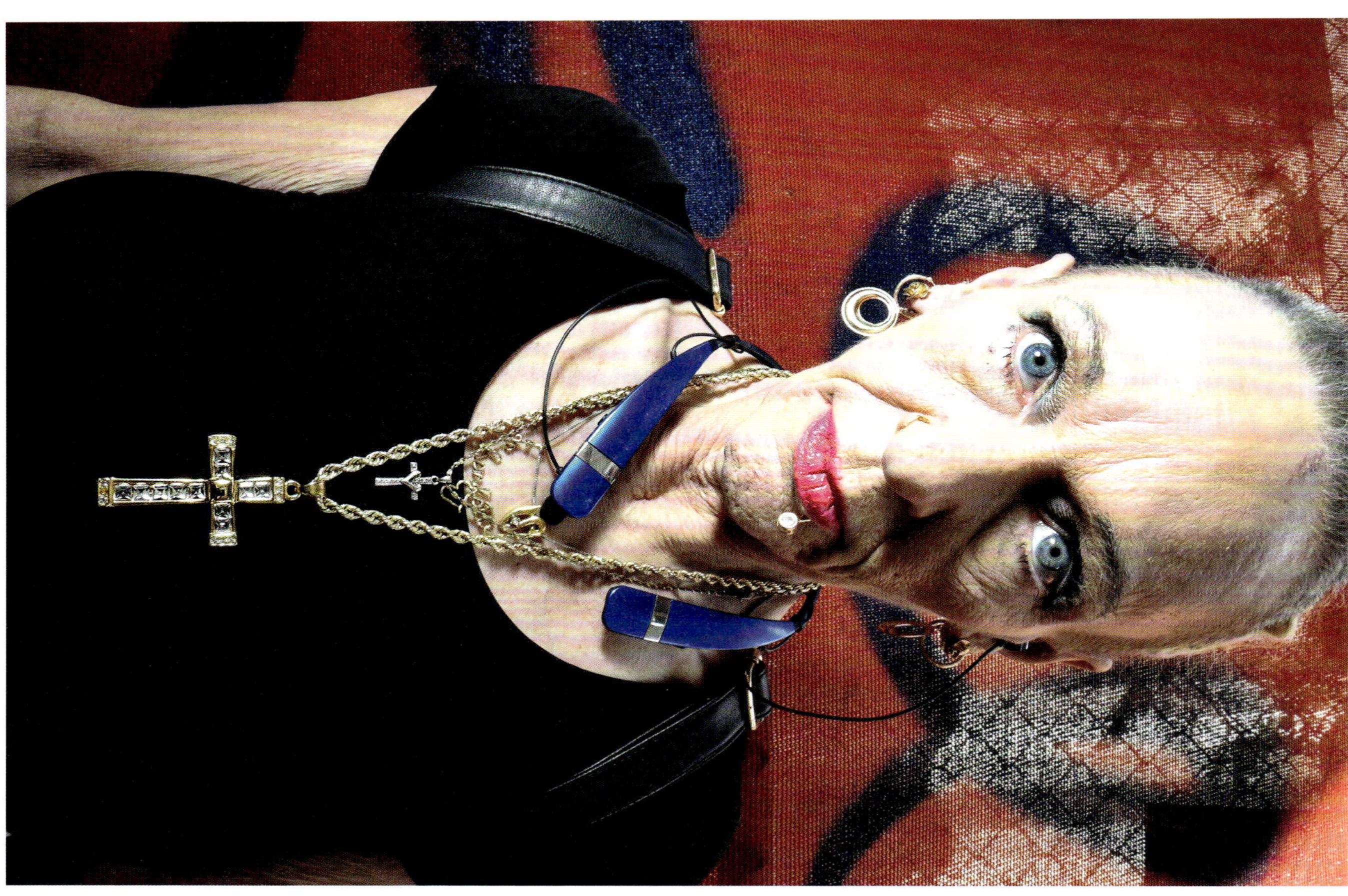

Commuter, Miami, Florida, 2017

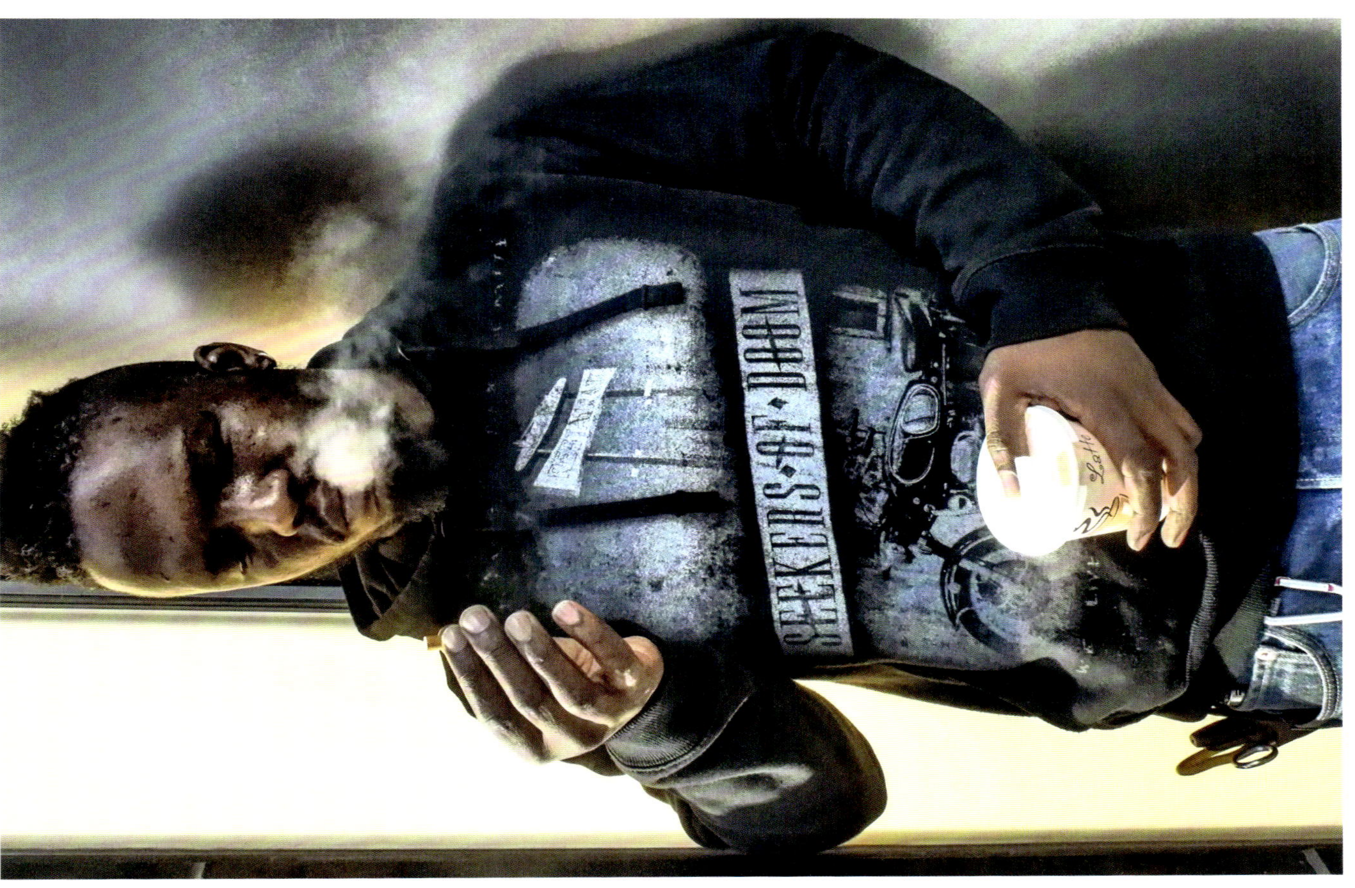

Construction Worker, NYC, 2014

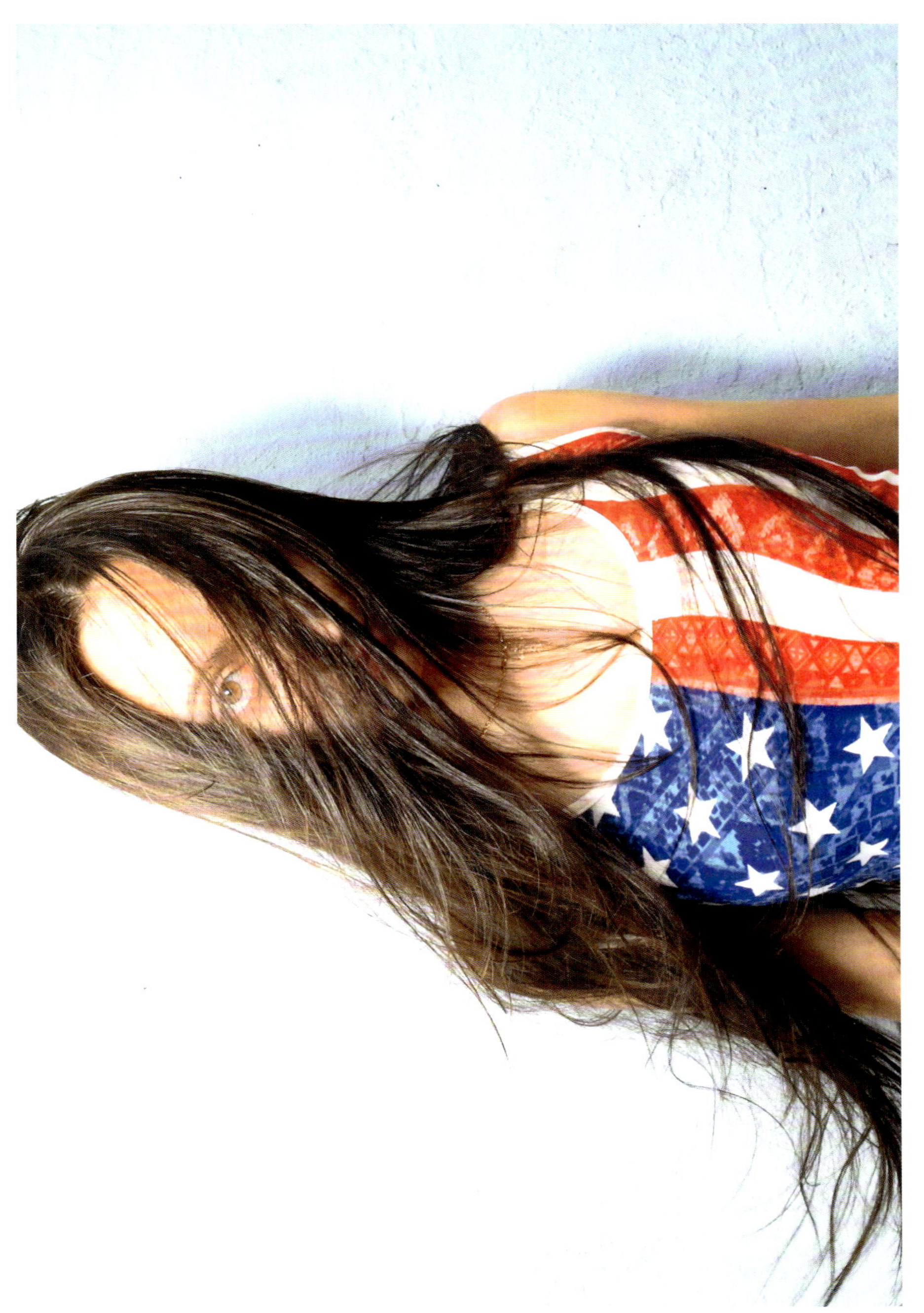

Independence Day, Miami, Florida, 2016

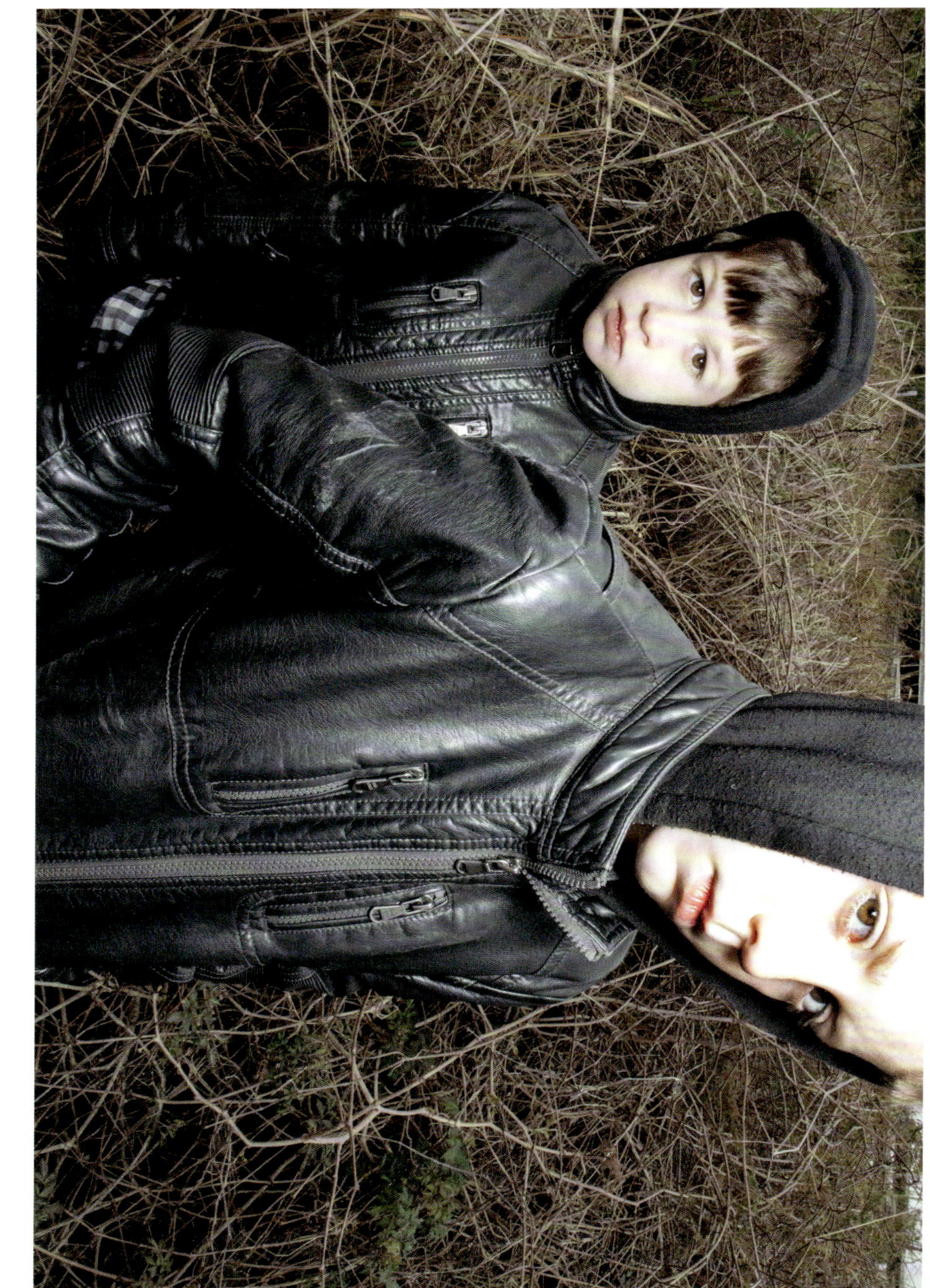

Brothers in a Field, Houston, Texas, 2018

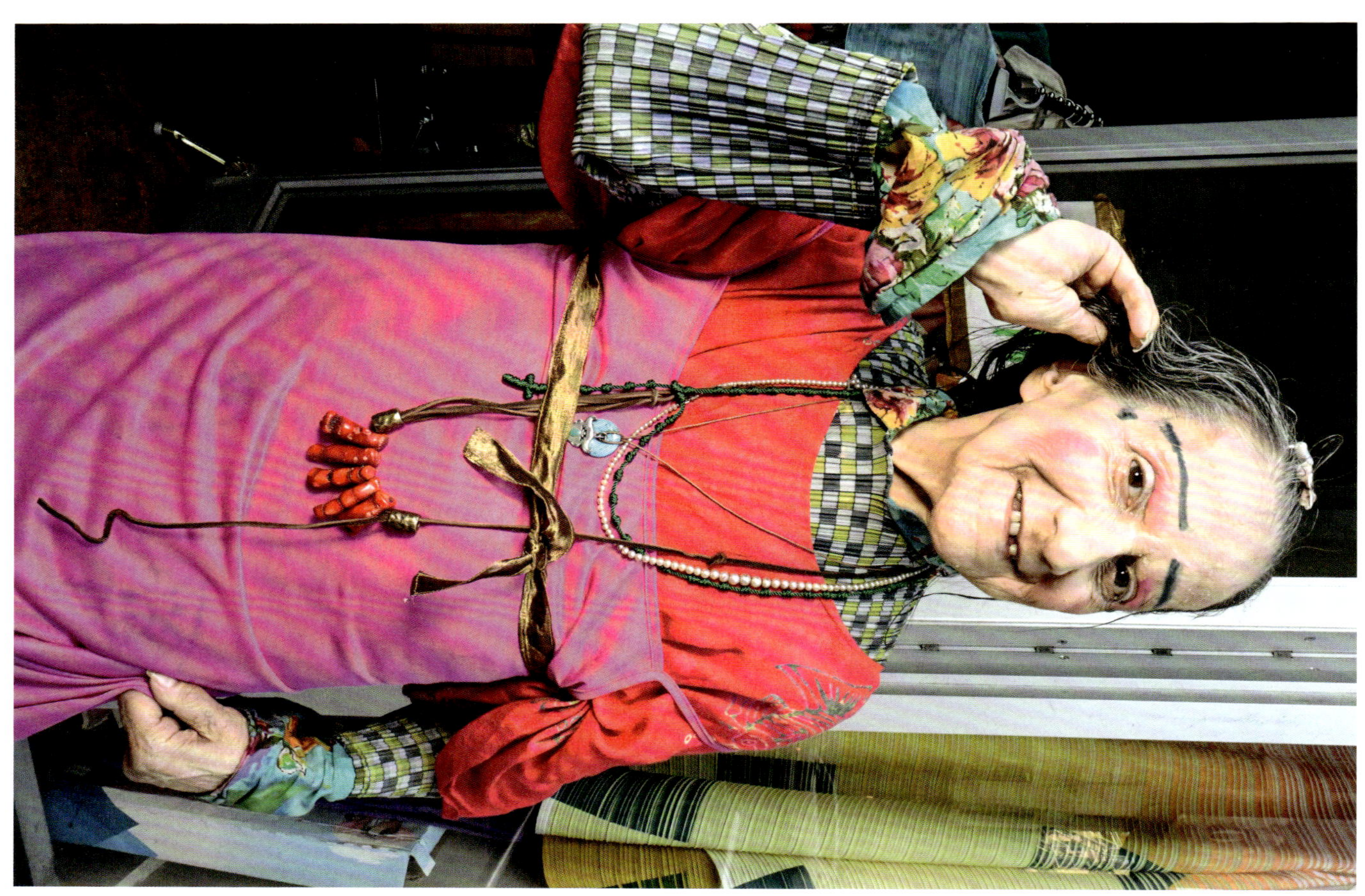

Dress Merchant, Chinatown, NYC, 2019

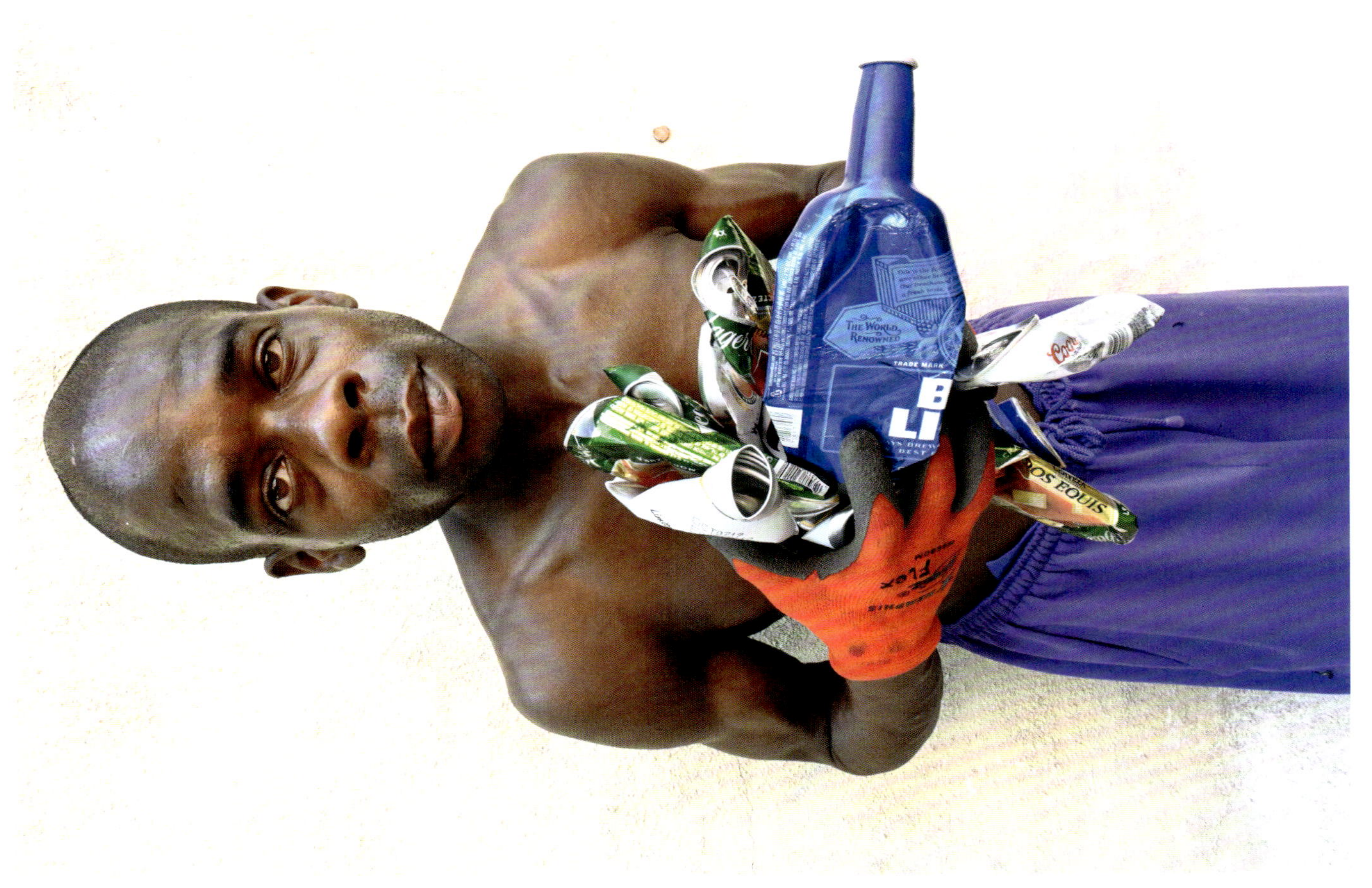

Marshall, Can Recycler, Houston, Texas, 2019

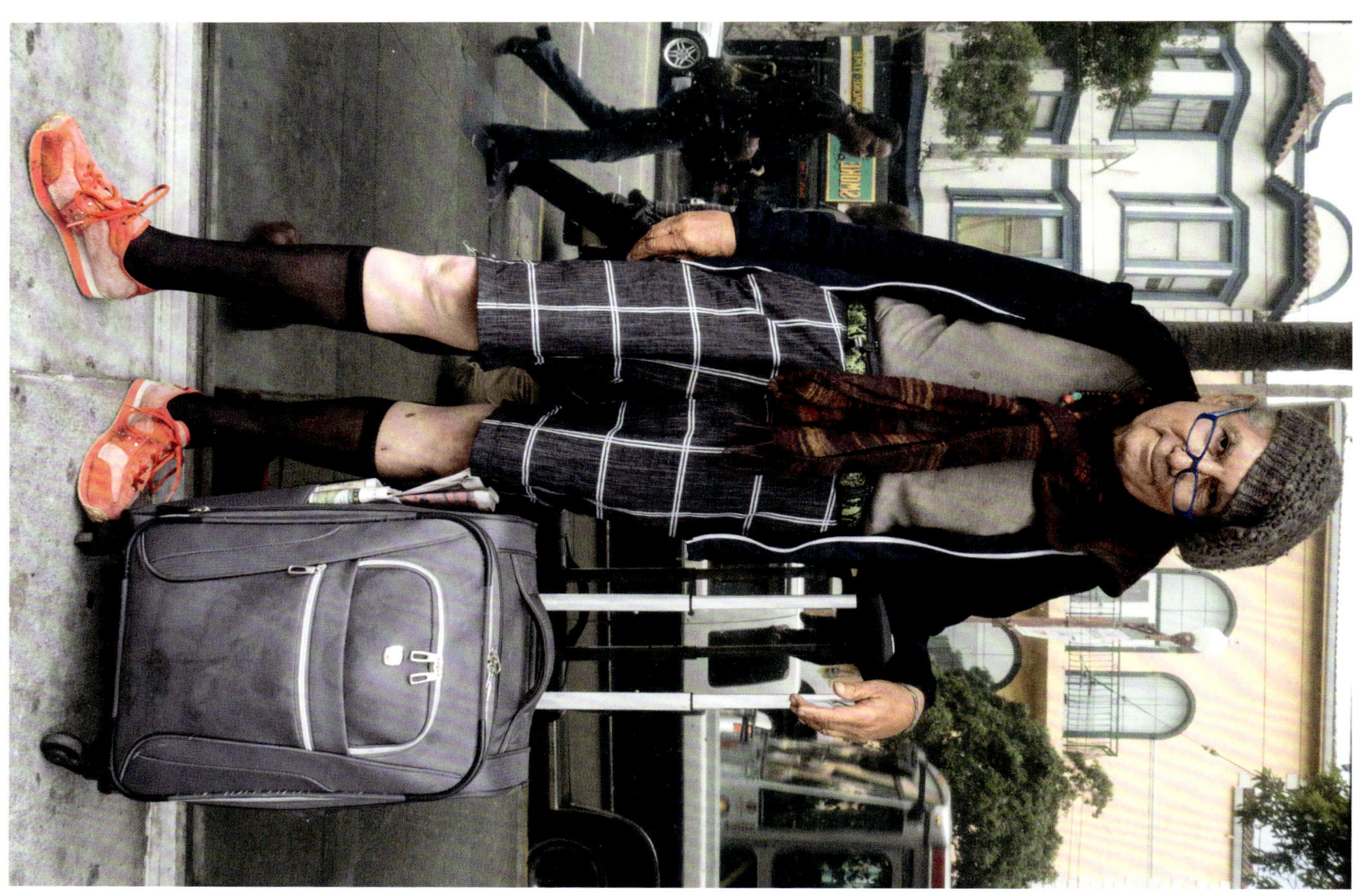

Chotak, Poet, San Francisco, California, 2015

Chris lives in a shelter and writes poetry. He asked me to please use his Tibetan name, Chotak. I asked him for a poem and he obliged: "I feel haunted and unwanted as the full moon begins to rise/In this deserted castle beneath the darkening skies."

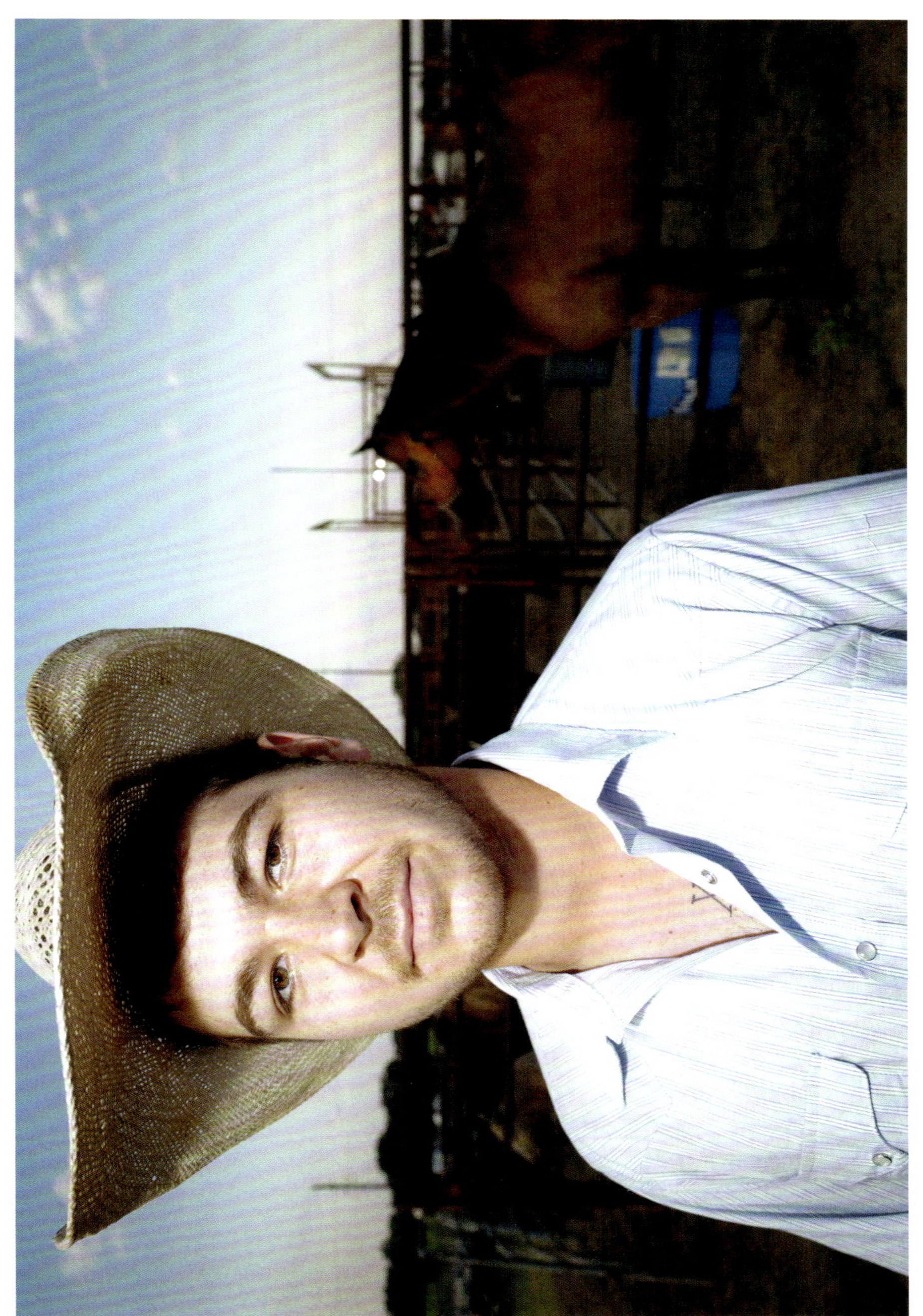

Kevin, Cowboy Bronc Rider, Columbus, Texas, 2021

Woman on LA Street, California, 2017

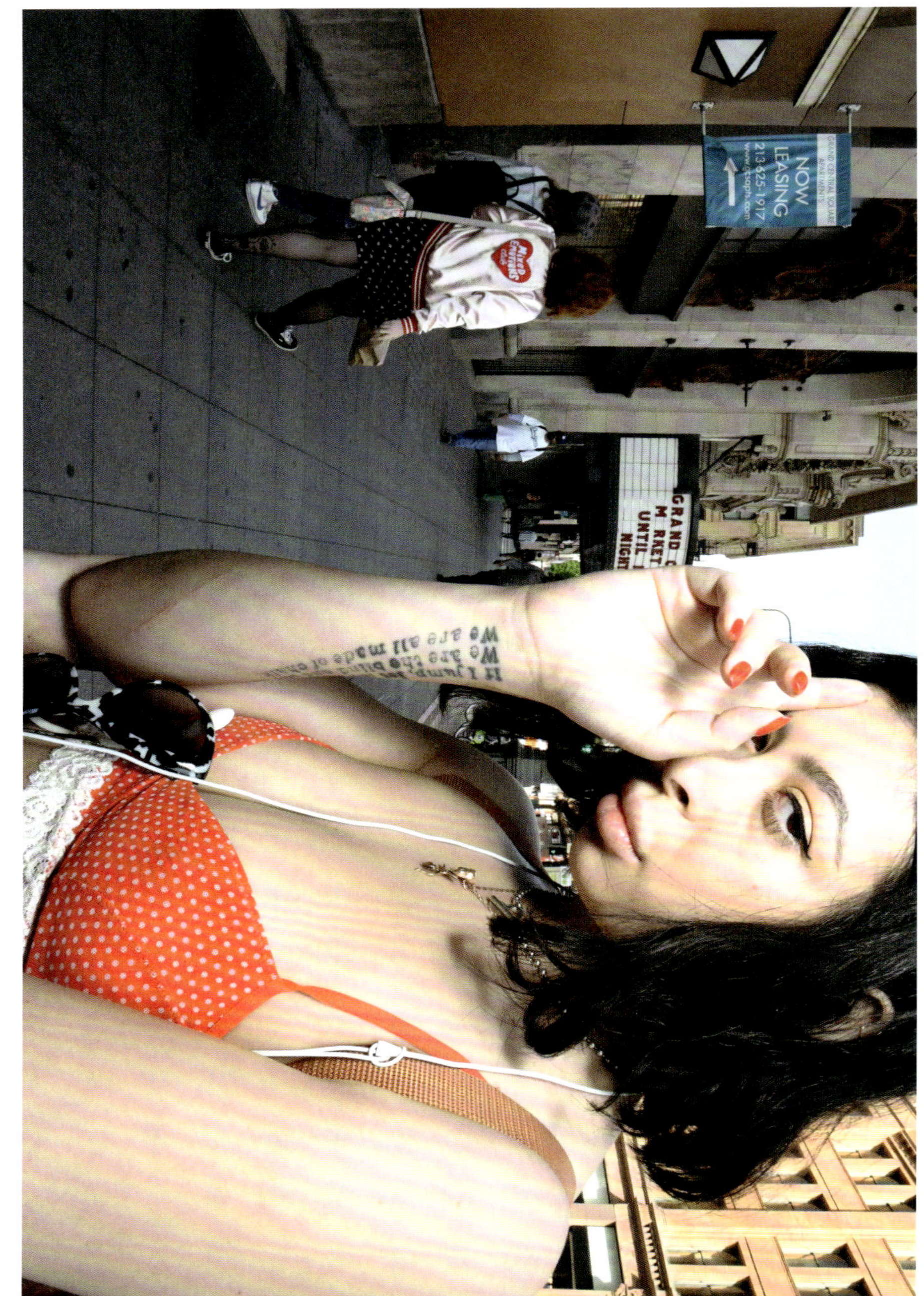
NOW
LEASING
213-425-1917
We are all made of
If I jump

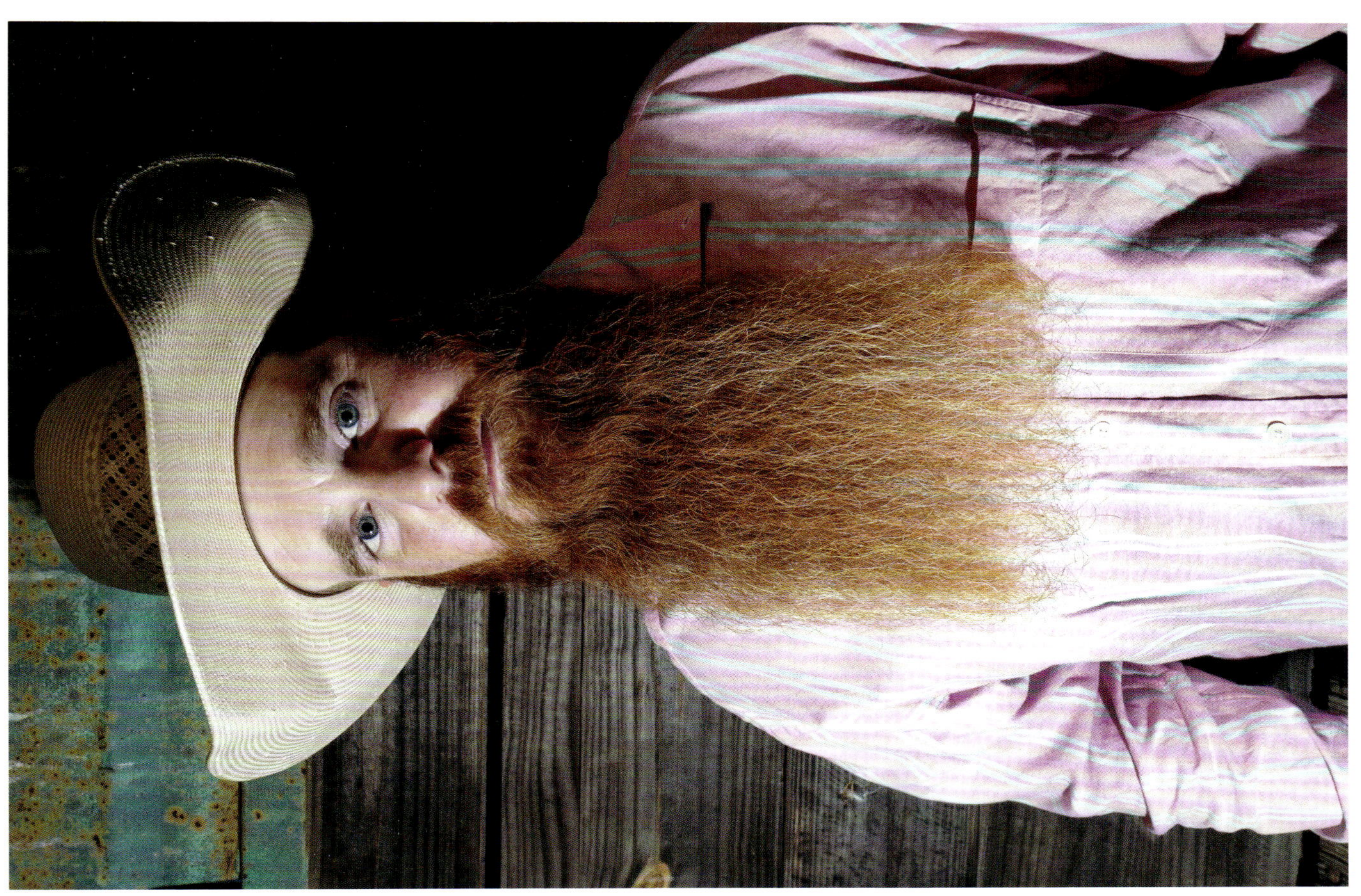

Johnathan, Rodeo Worker, New Braunfels, Texas, 2021

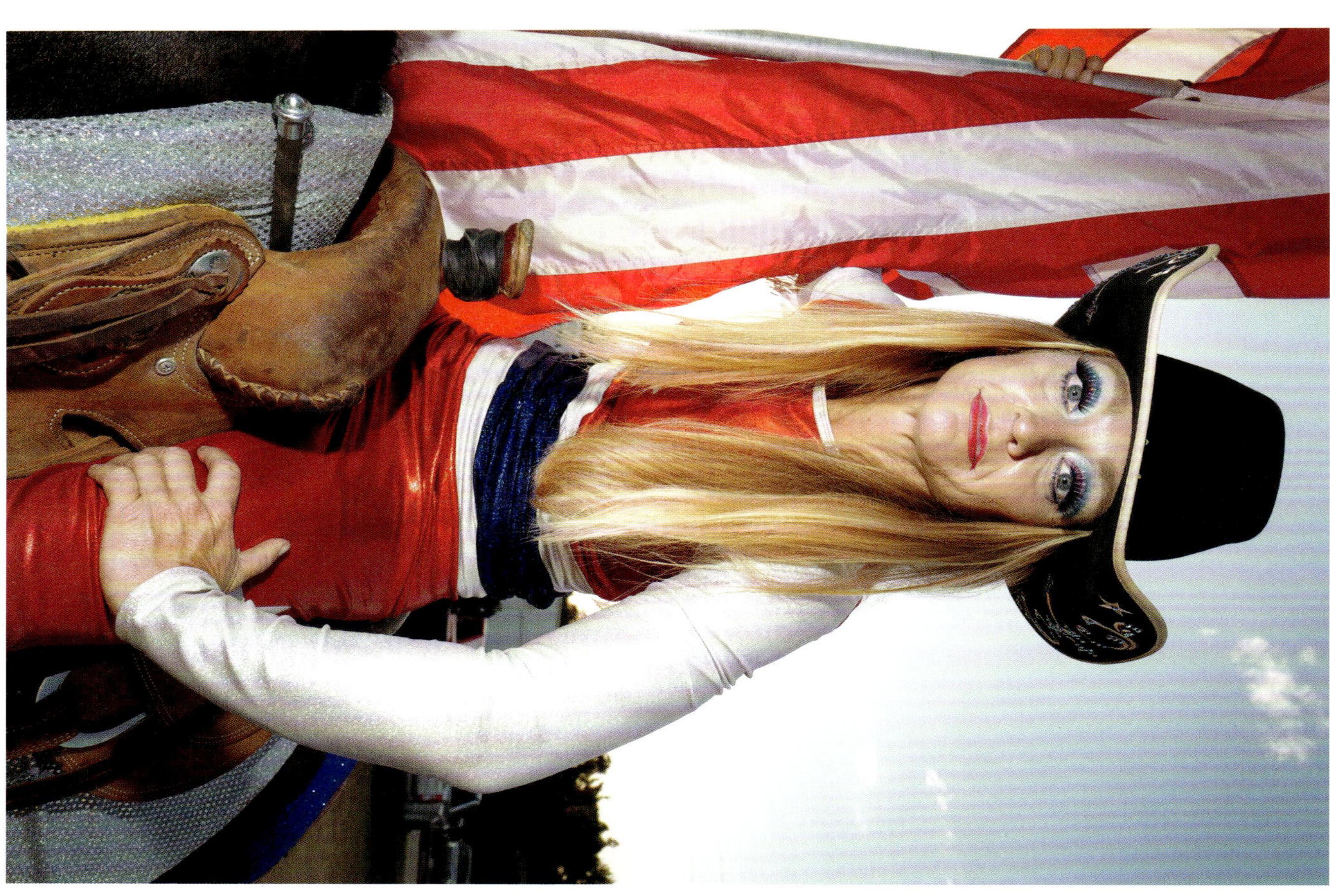

Ginger, Trick Rider, Brenham, Texas, 2021

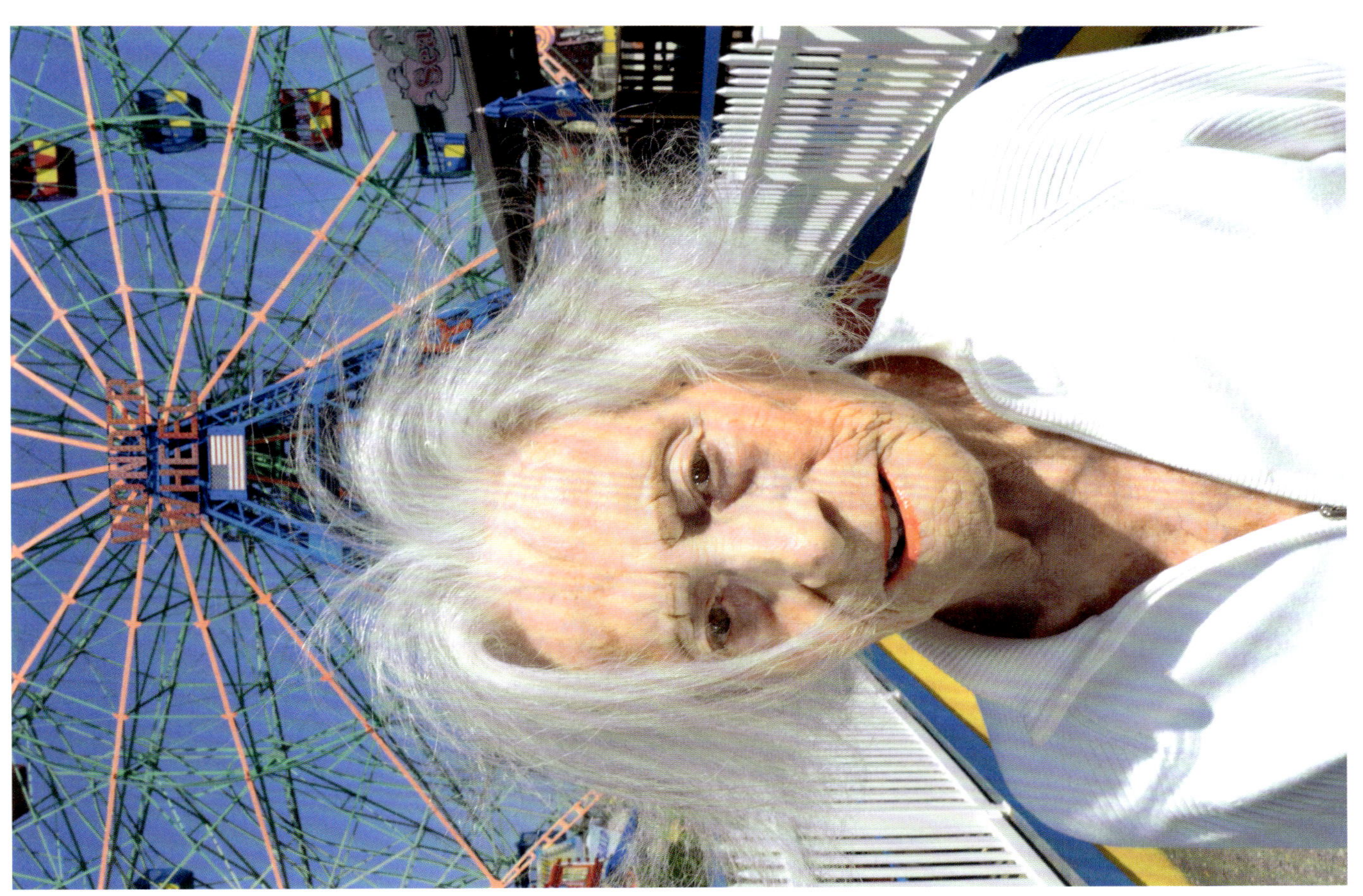

Lily, Senior Citizen at Coney Island, NYC, 2018

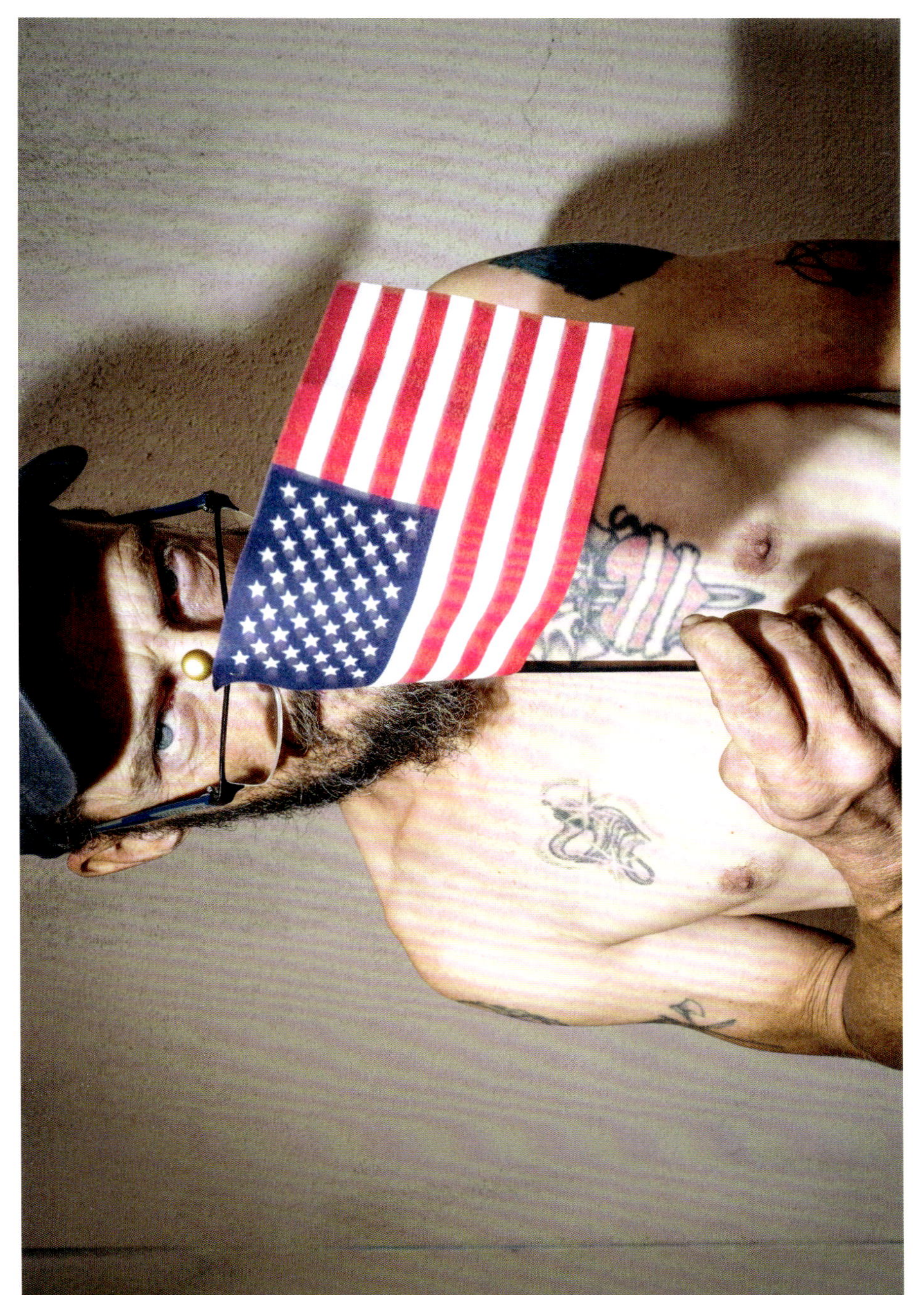

Election, Houston, Texas, 2020

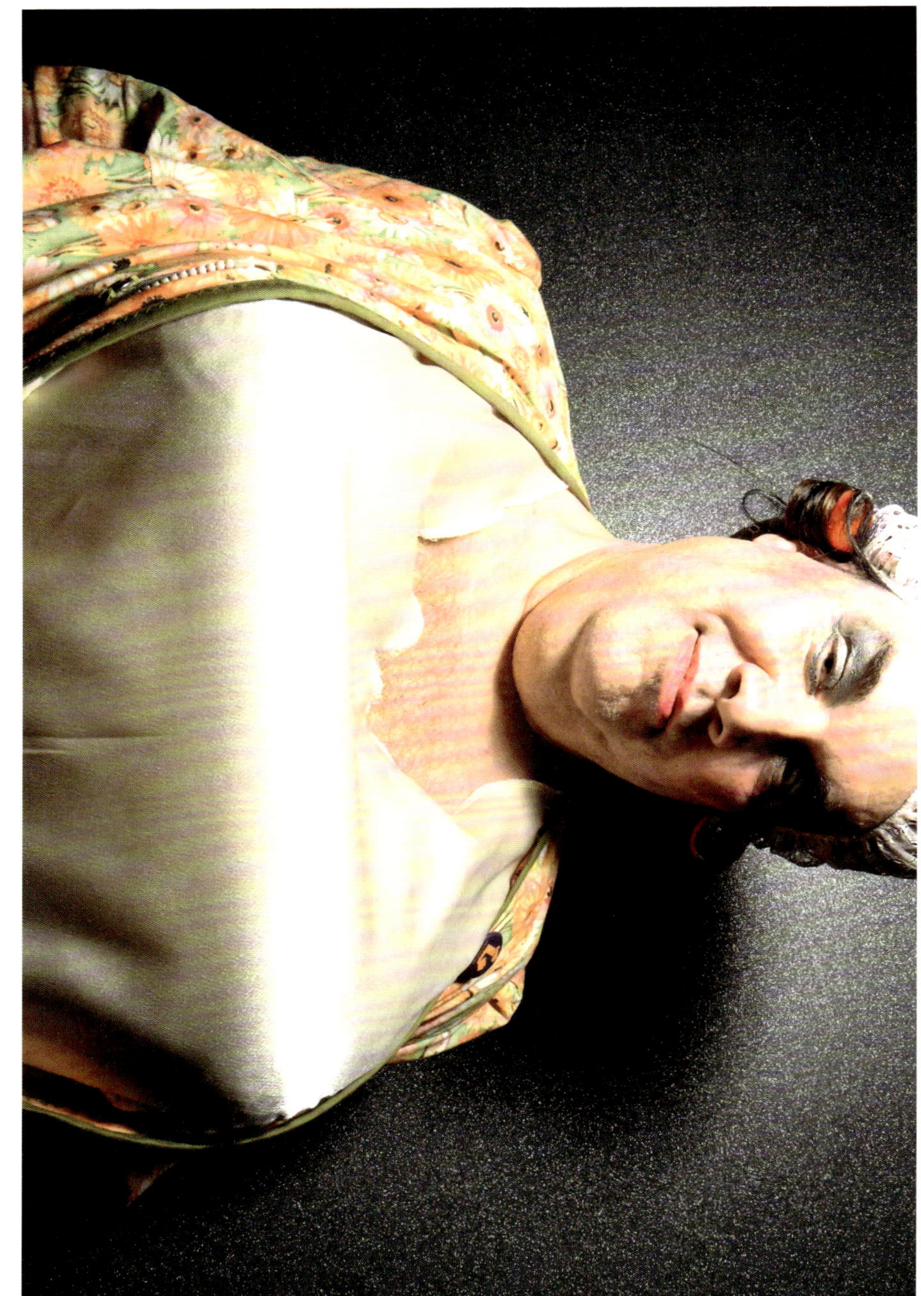

Man in Drag, Houston, Texas, 2017

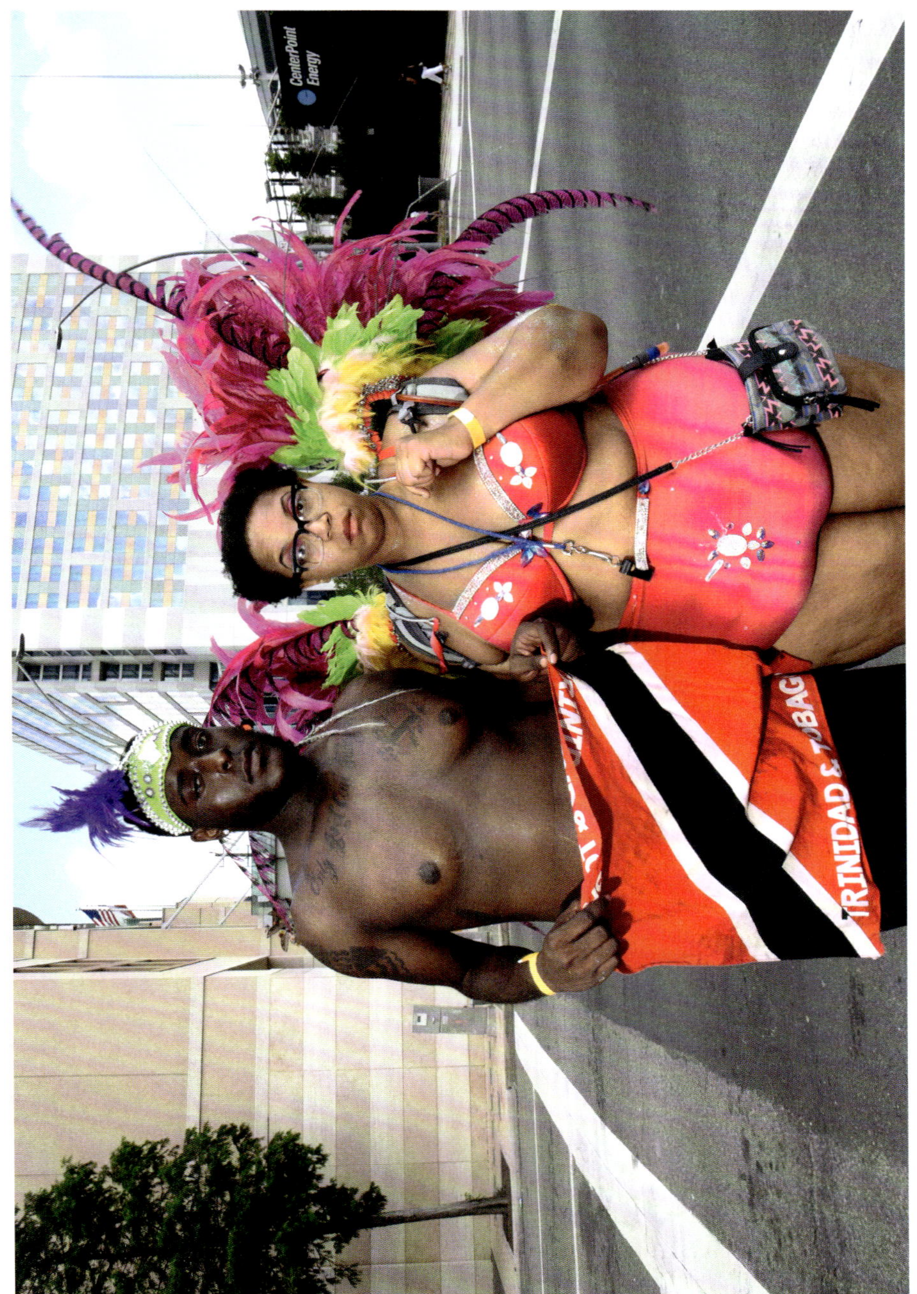

Couple Dressed for a Festival, Houston, Texas, 2016

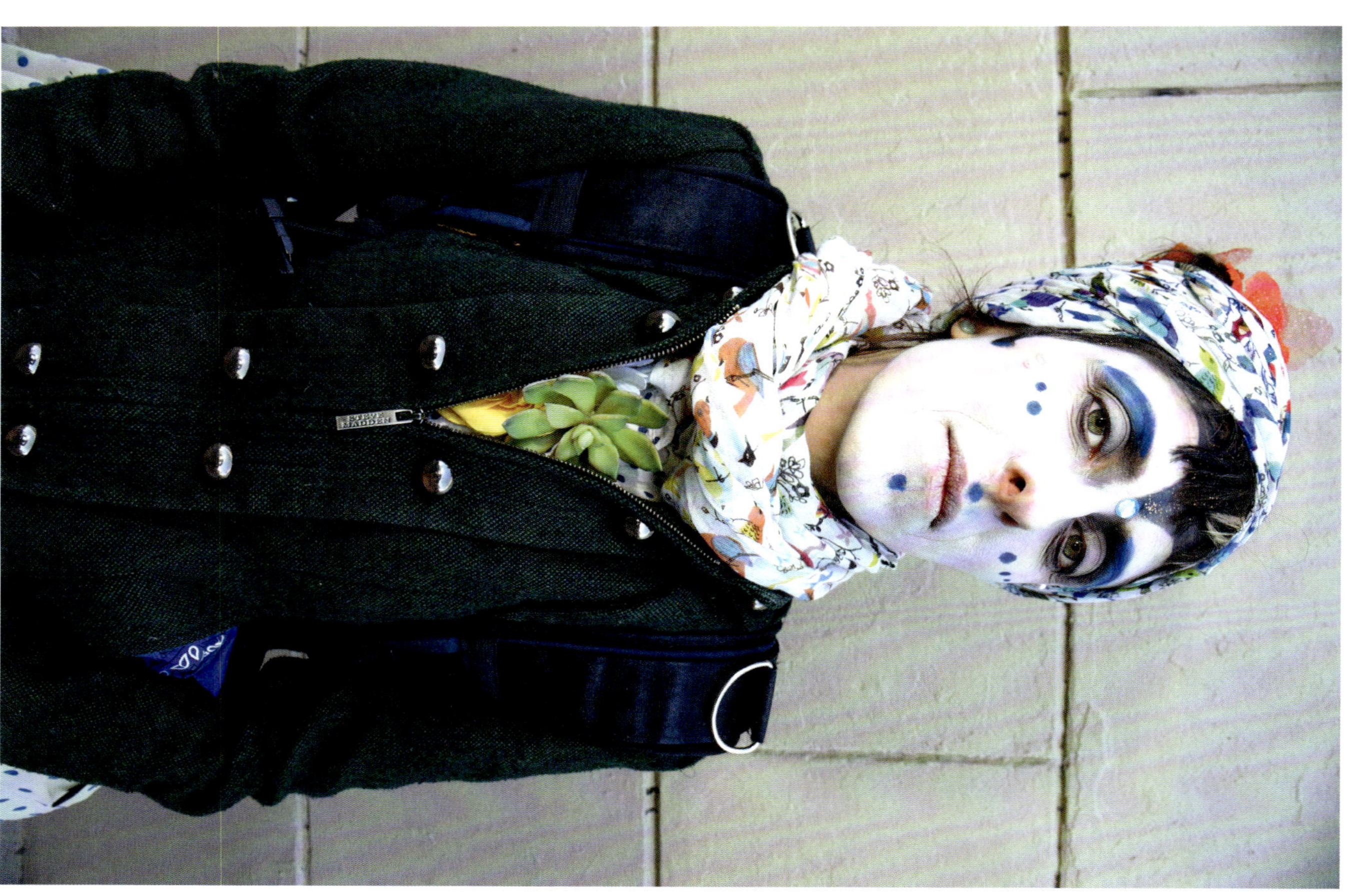

Pixie Woman, New Orleans, Louisiana, 2016

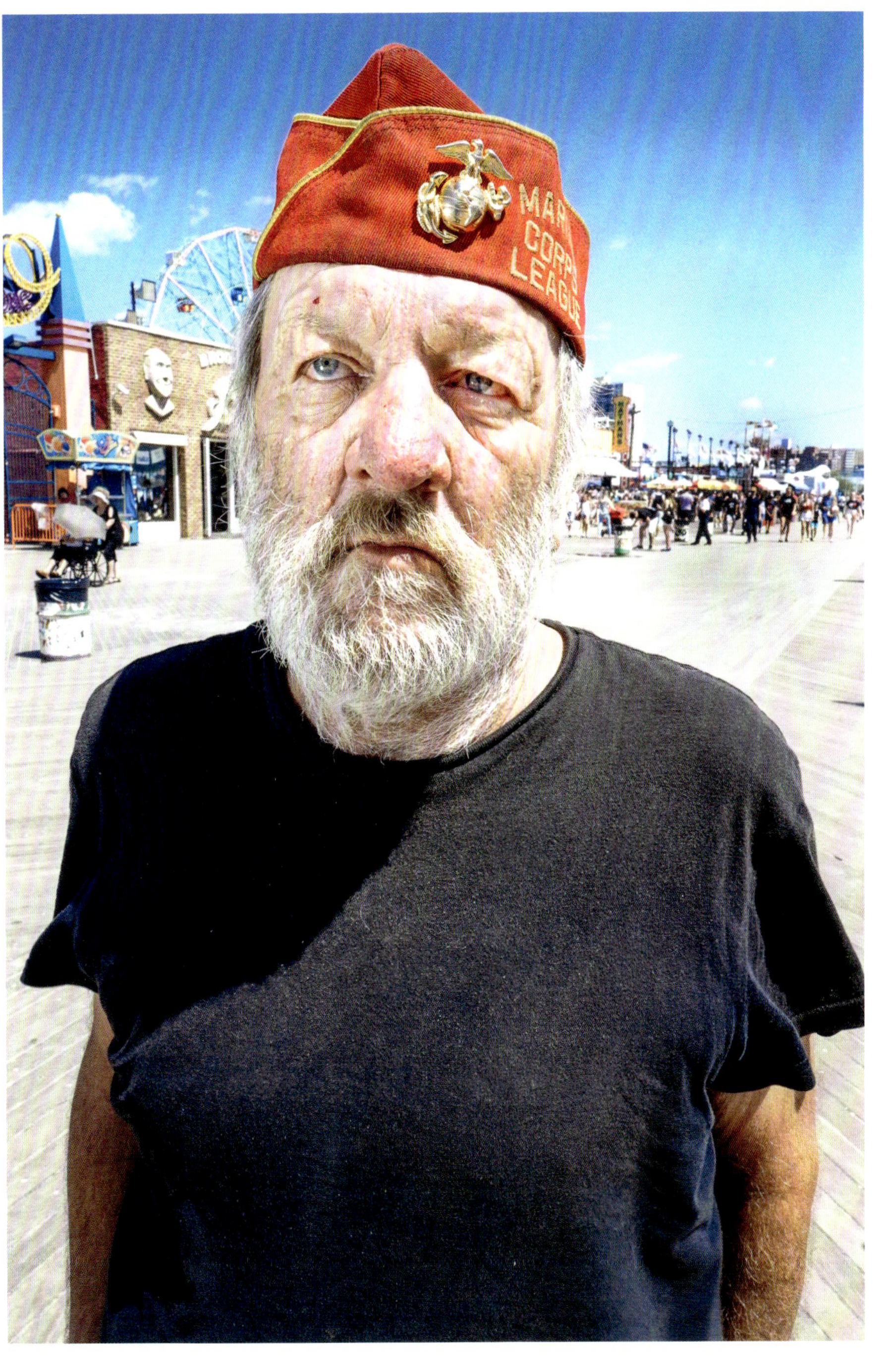

Dave, Veteran, Coney Island, NYC, 2018

This photograph
was made the day
"open carry" was
legalized in Texas. I
asked Scott what he
thought about gun
control and he told
me, "Gun control is
knowing where your
gun is pointed at
all times."

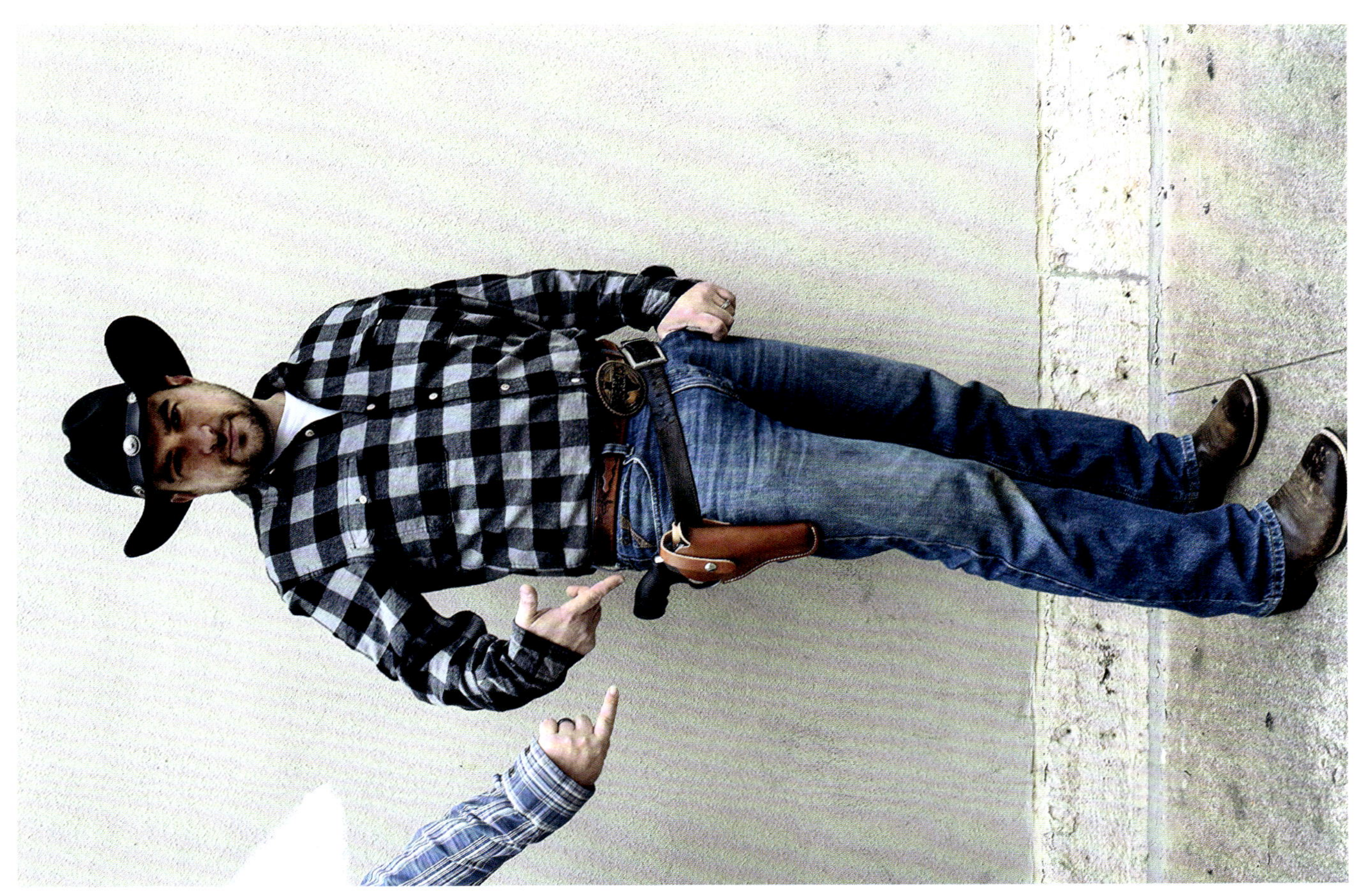

Scott with His Pistol, Austin, Texas, 2016

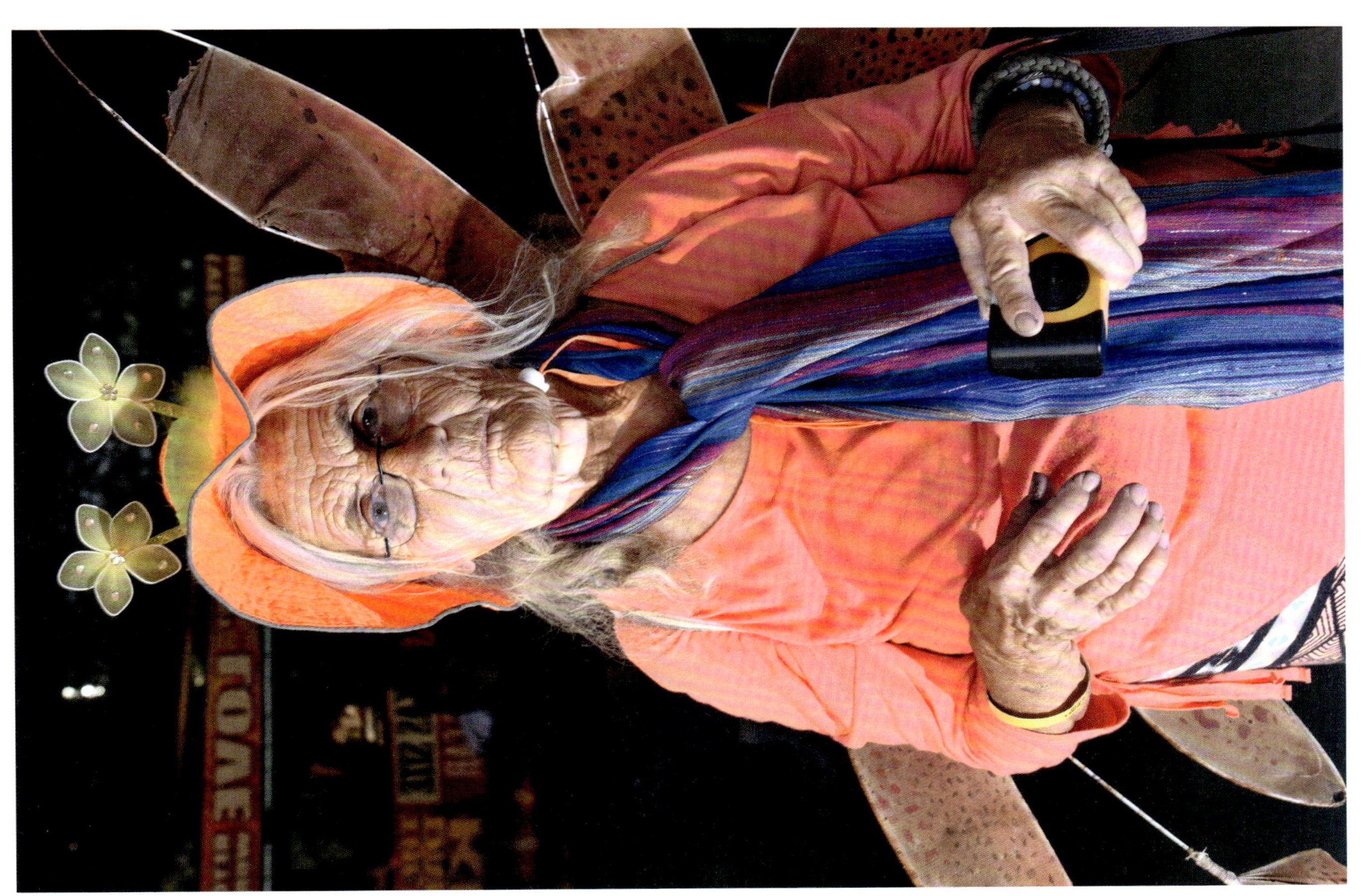

Woman at the Art Car Ball. Houston, Texas. 2016

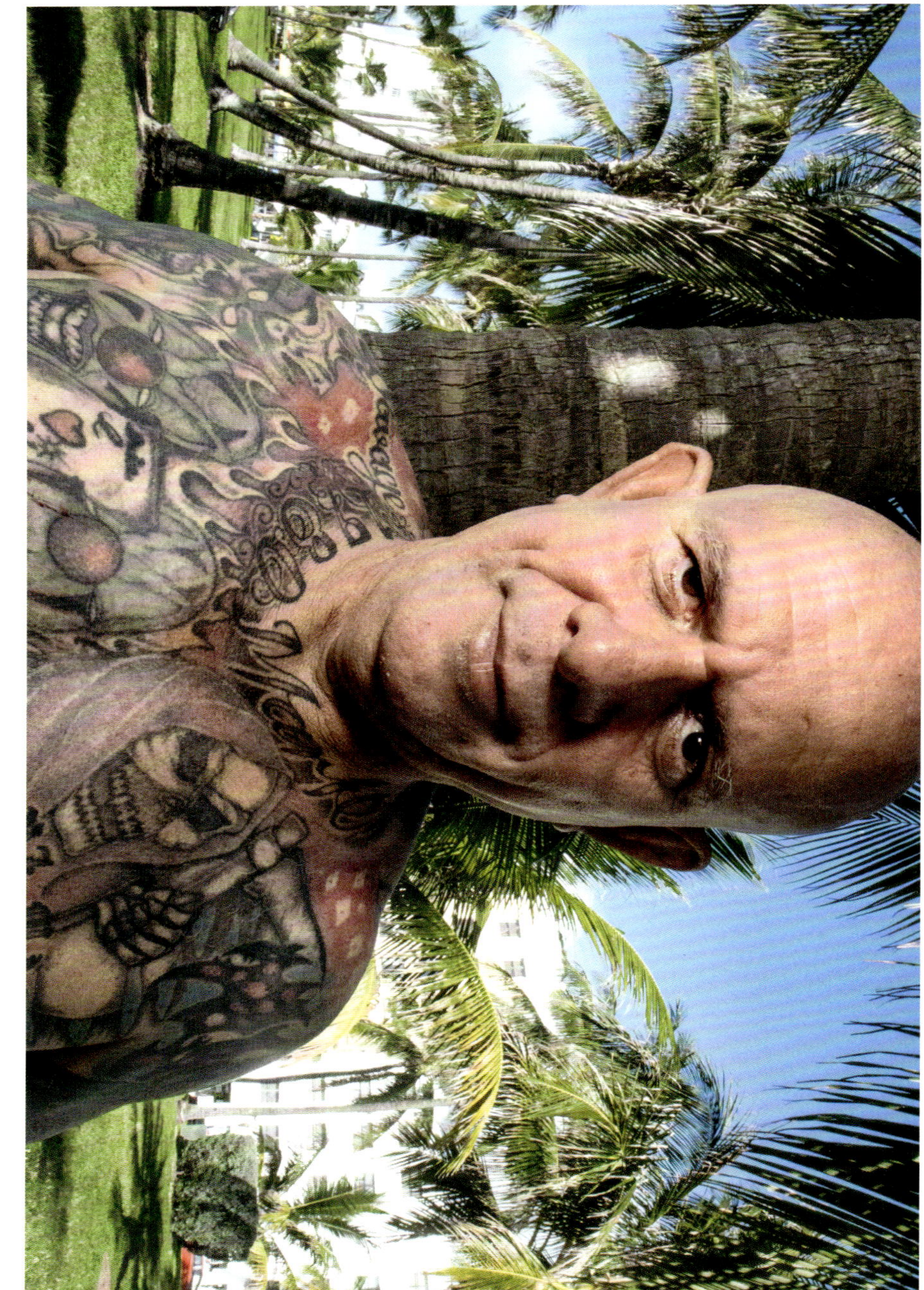

Tattooed Man, Miami, Florida, 2017

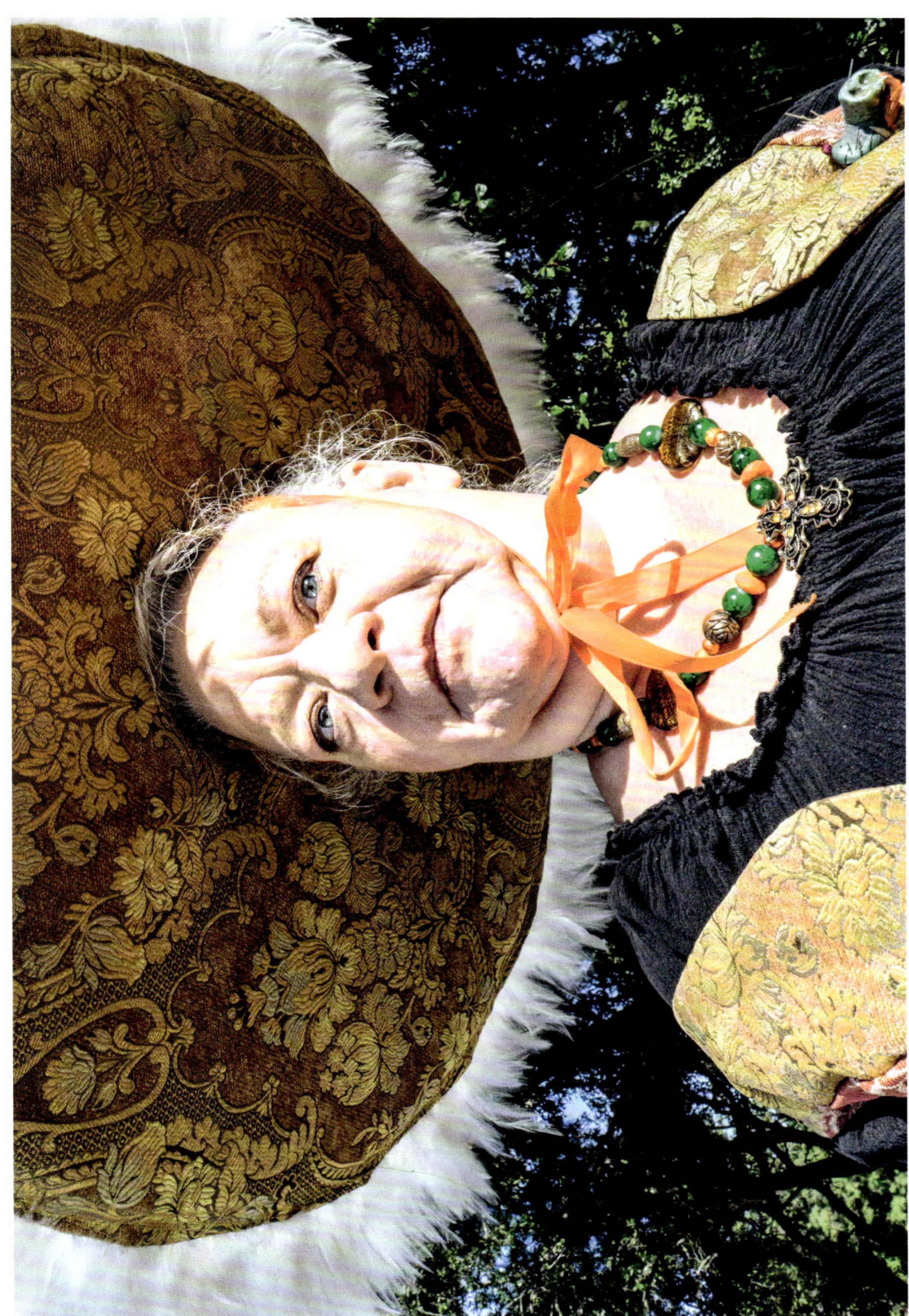

Woman in Large Hat, Houston, Texas, 2017

I first met Dorothy (Dot) and Bernard in 2014. I photographed them over the next few years, through the ups and downs of their relationship. Shown here, Dorothy has just told me that they are trying to get an apartment and may end their wandering ways for a while.

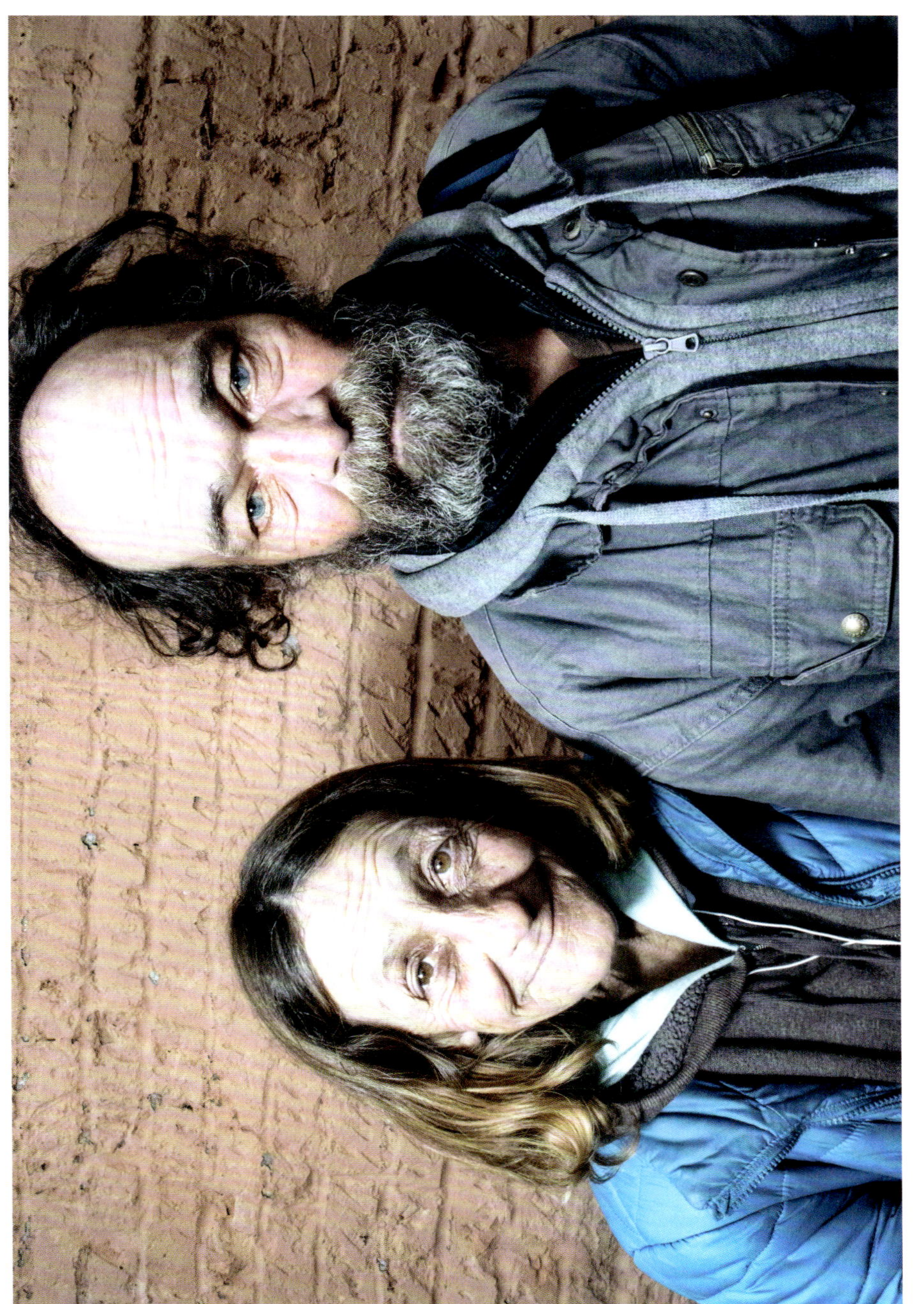

Dorothy and Bernard in Happy Times, Houston, Texas, 2018

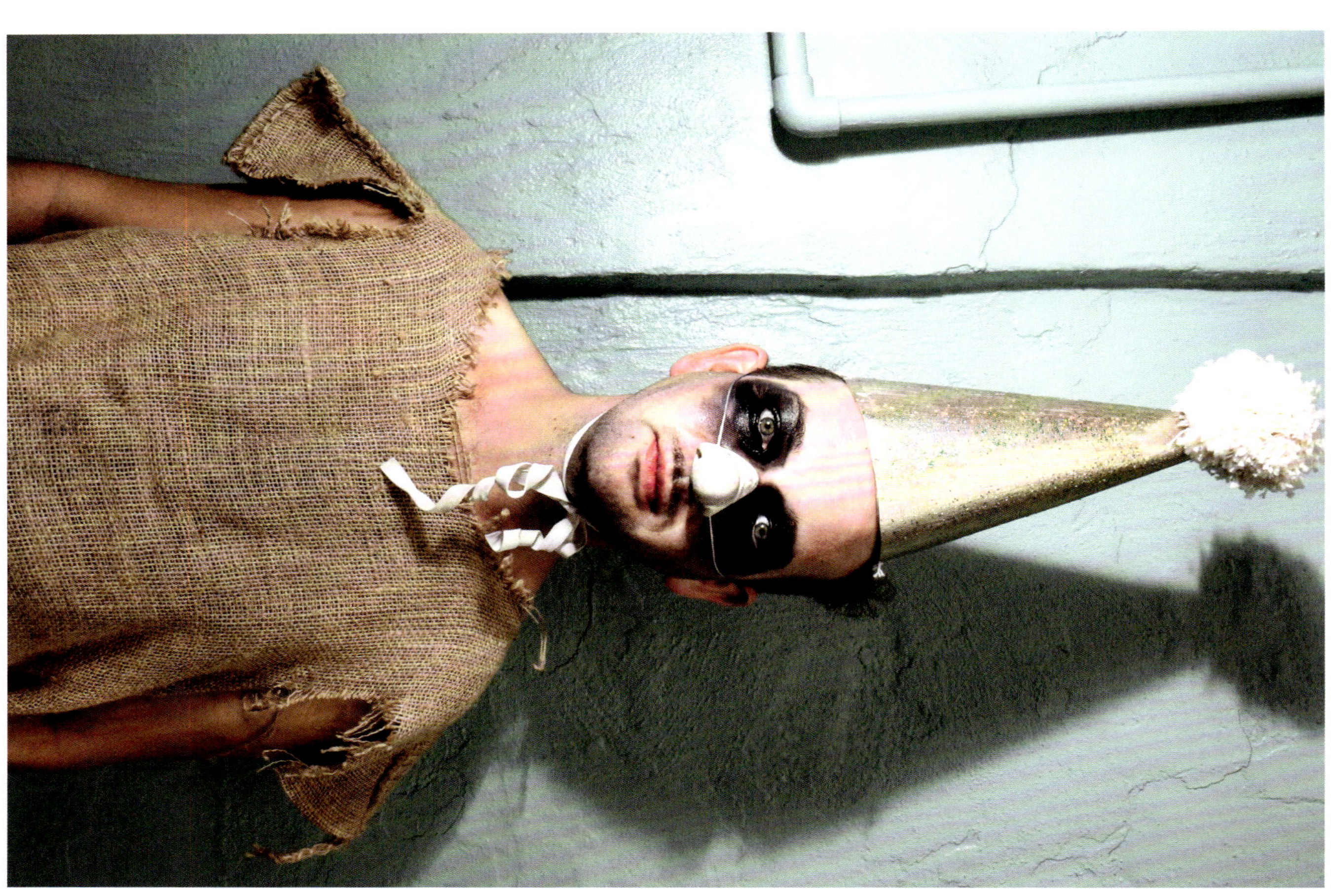

Robin, Street Musician, New Orleans, Louisiana, 2018

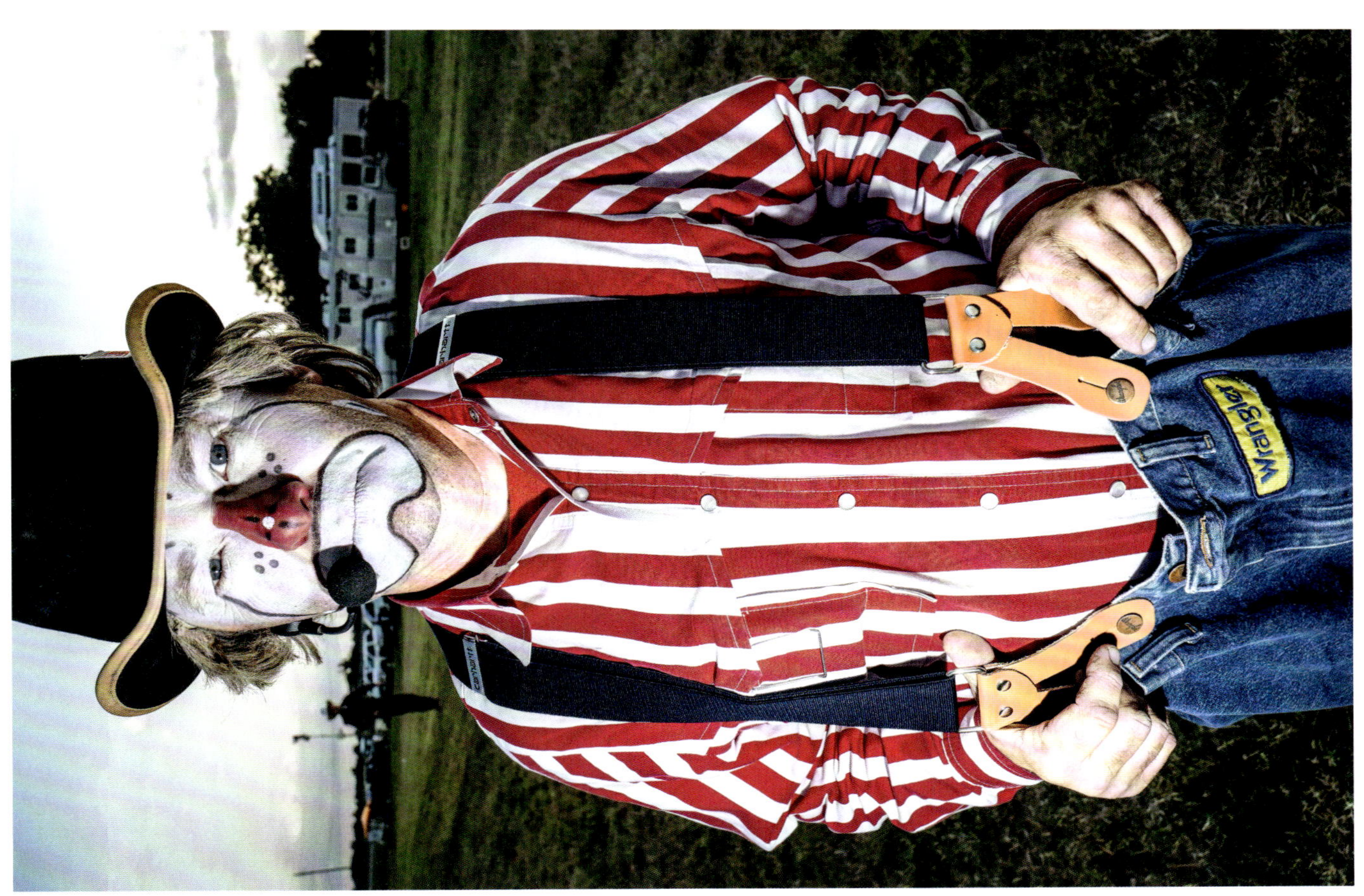

Ronald, Rodeo Clown, Columbus, Texas, 2021

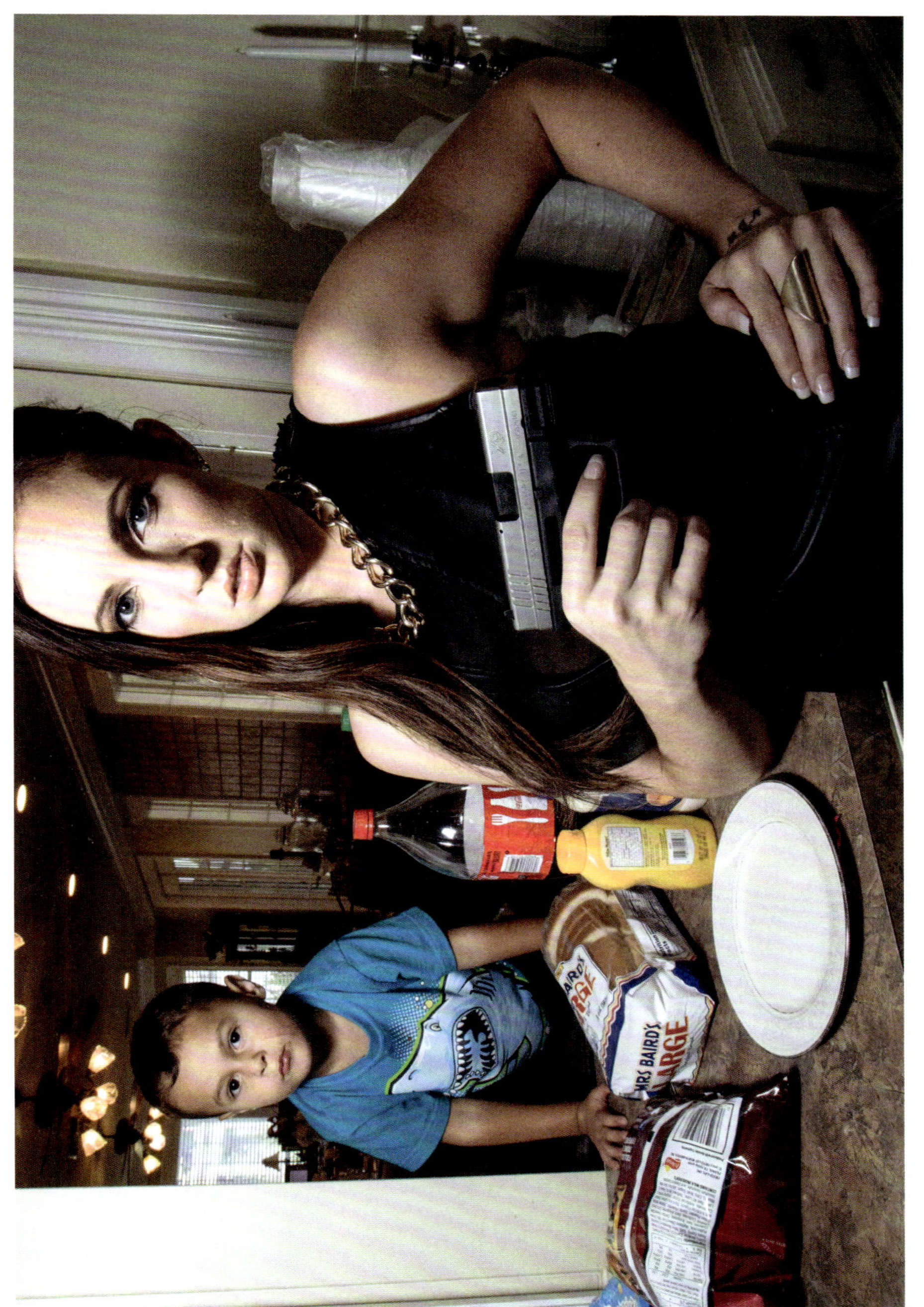

Woman with Her Pistol, Needville, Texas, 2016

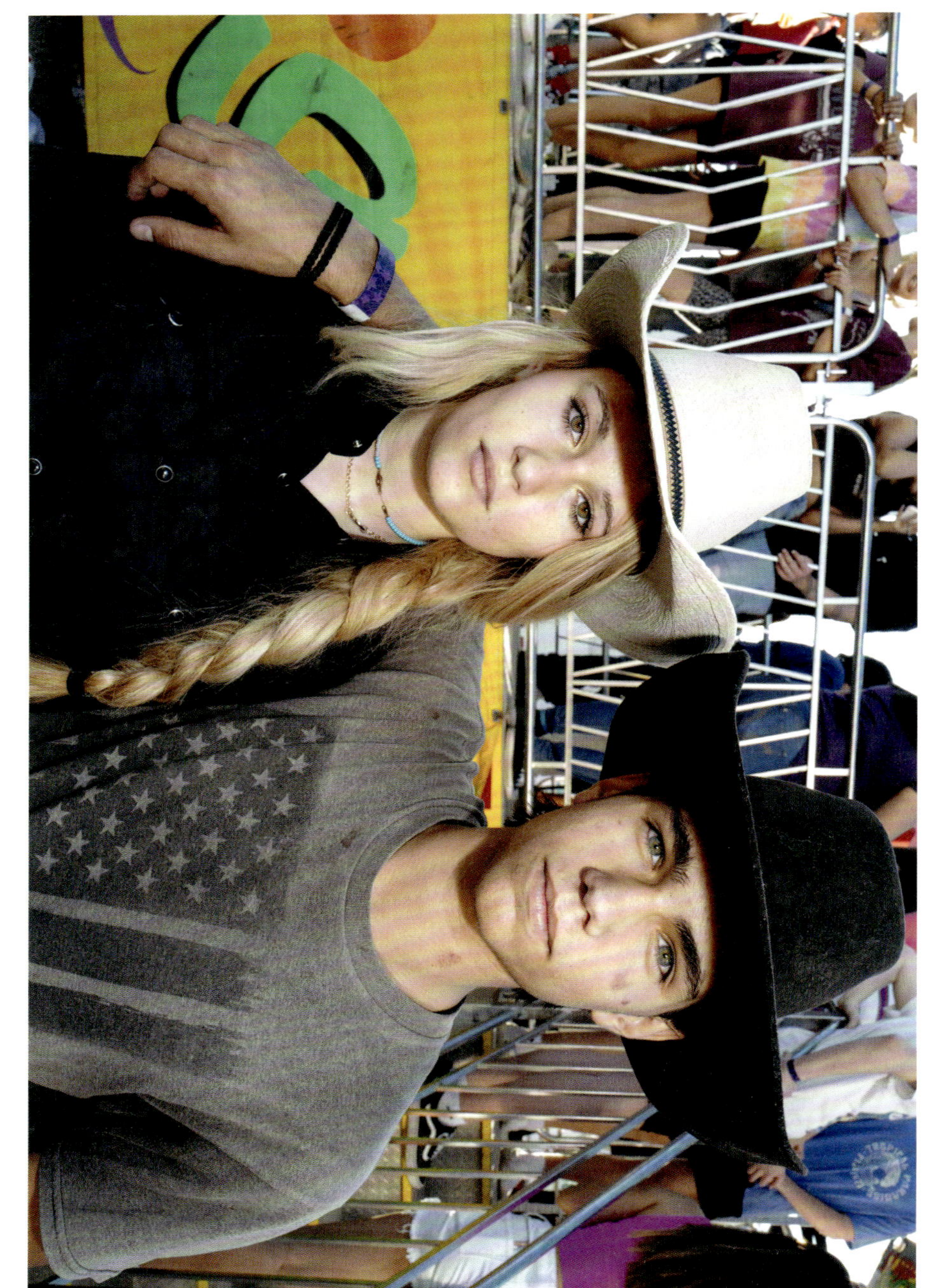

Mayce and Tristan at a Rodeo and County Fair, New Braunfels, Texas, 2021

Mayce is a barrel racer; Tristan rides bulls. Anyone can wear a cowboy hat, but these two are the REAL DEAL, growing up around farming, ranching, and rodeo.

Bill Cunningham said, "The best fashion show is definitely on the street. Always has been, and always will be."

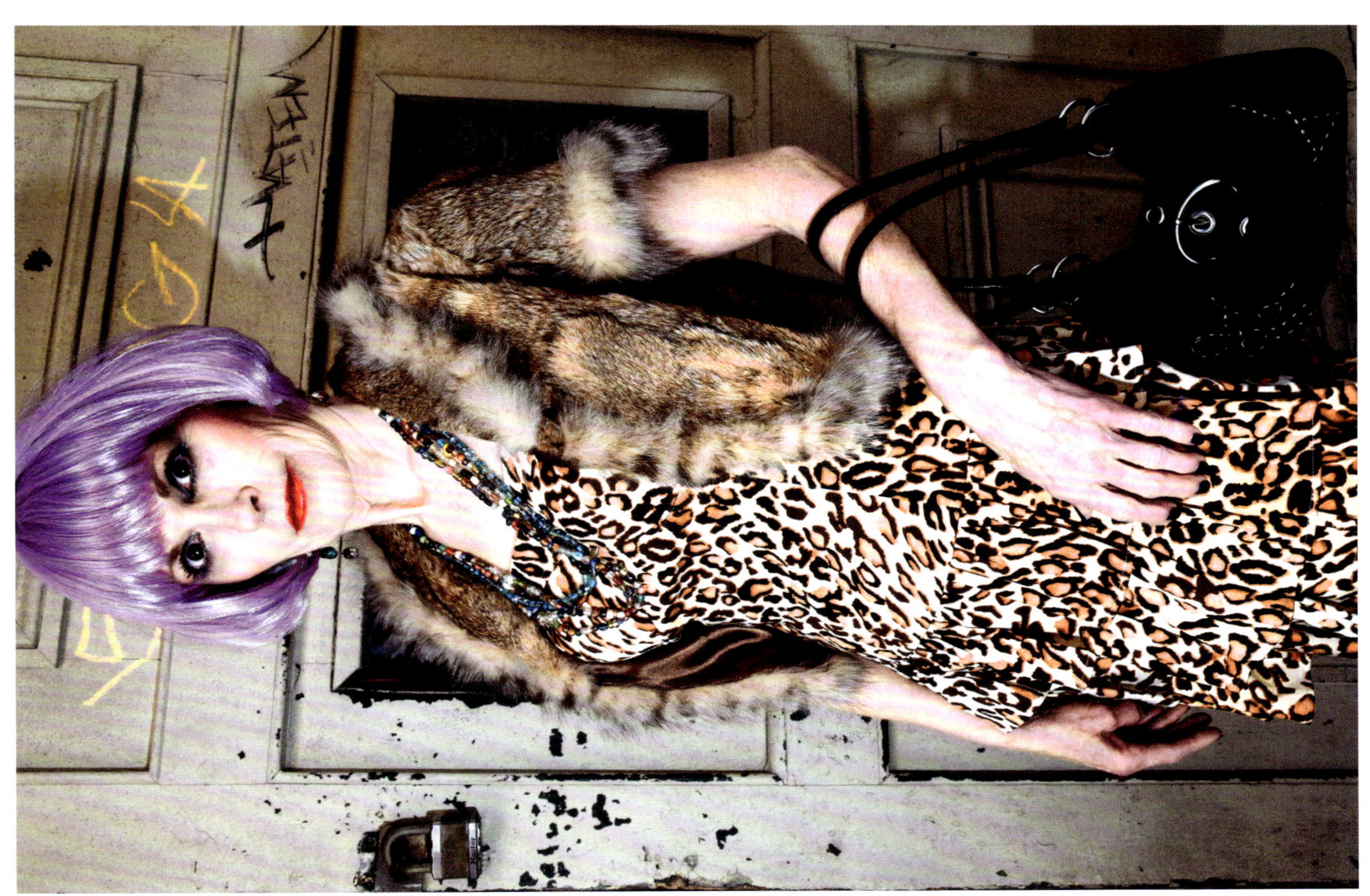

Woman with Purple Hair, New Orleans, Louisiana, 2016

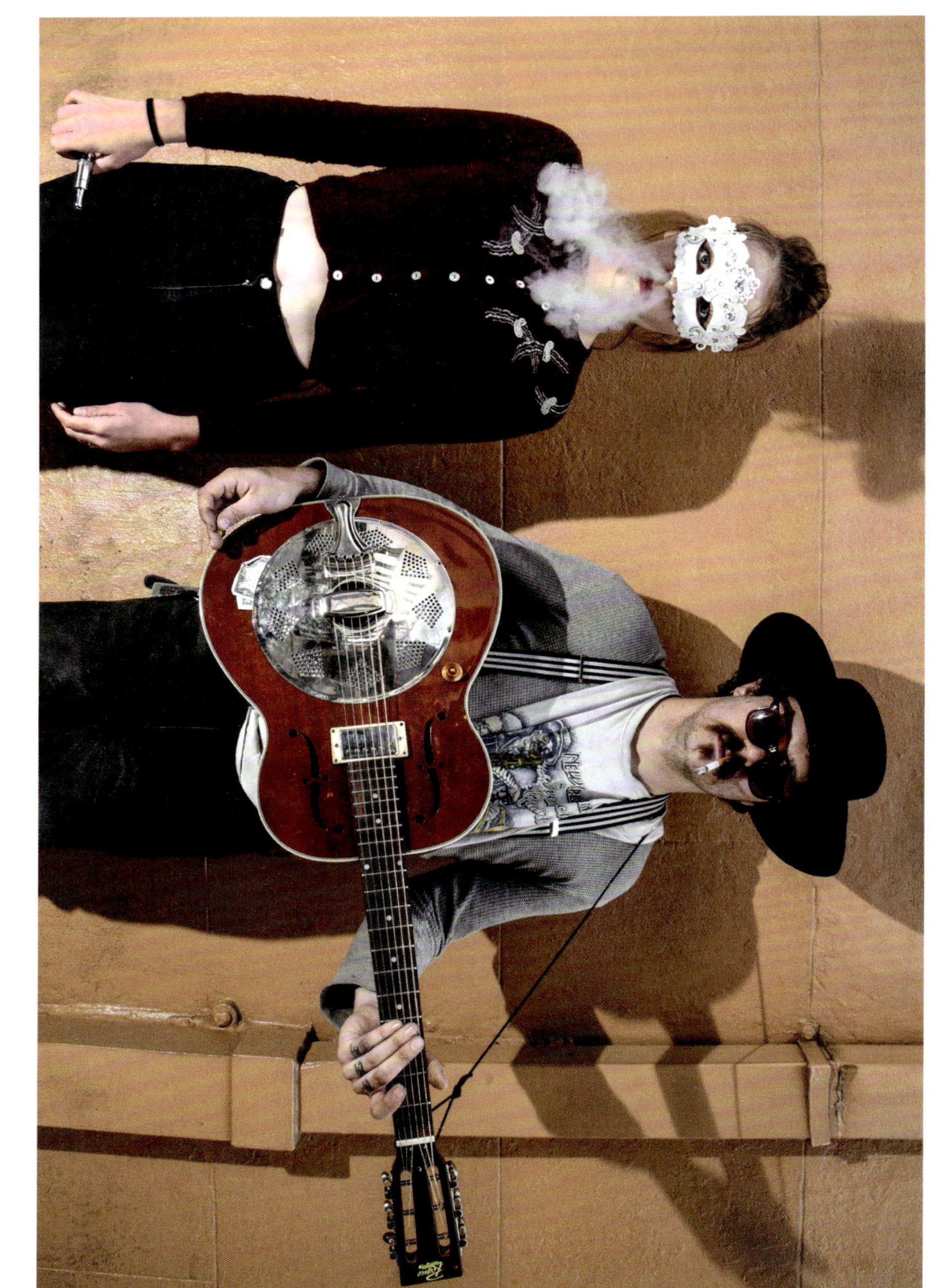

Buskers in the French Quarter, New Orleans, Louisiana, 2016

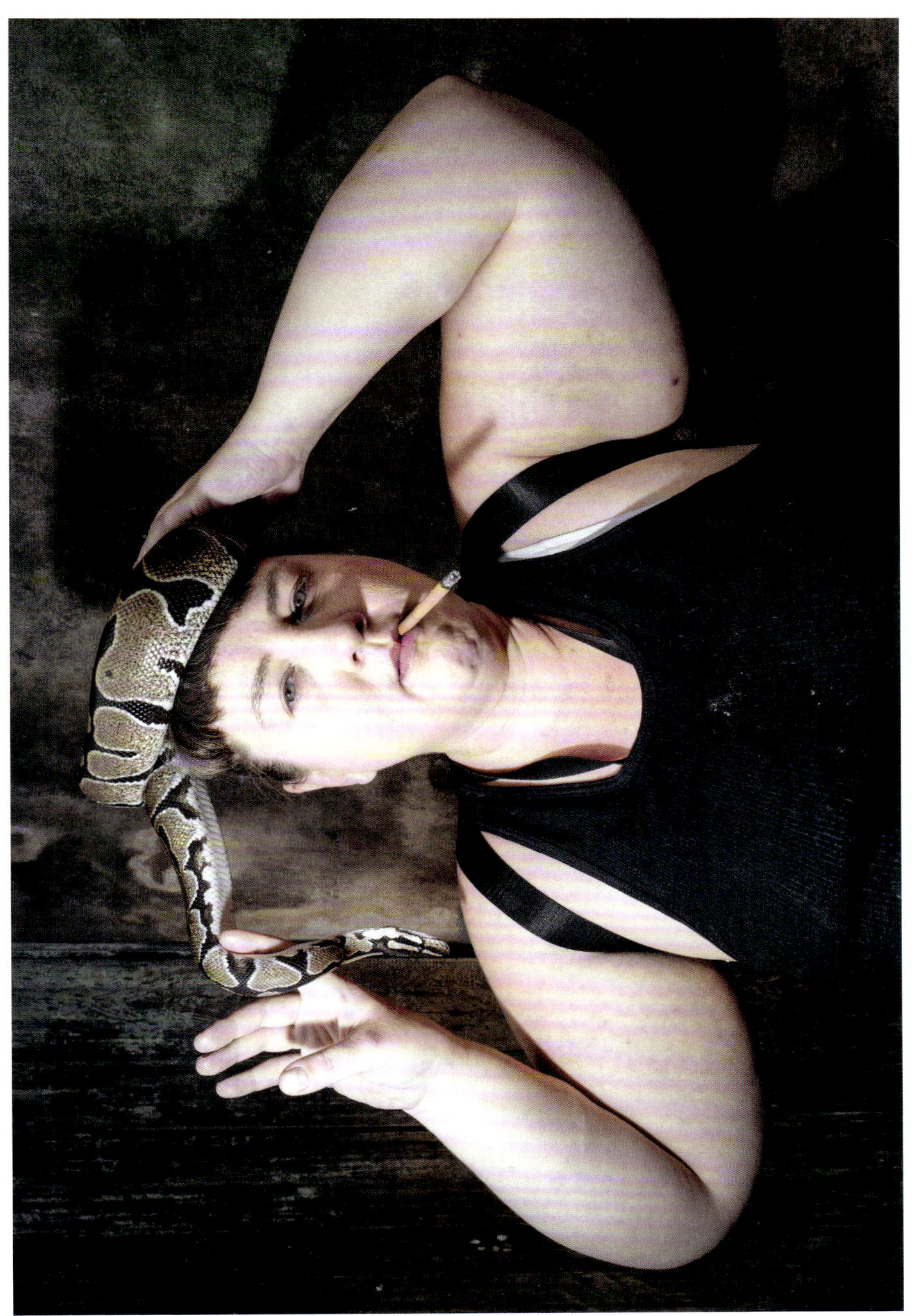

Woman with Her Snake, New Orleans, Louisiana, 2020

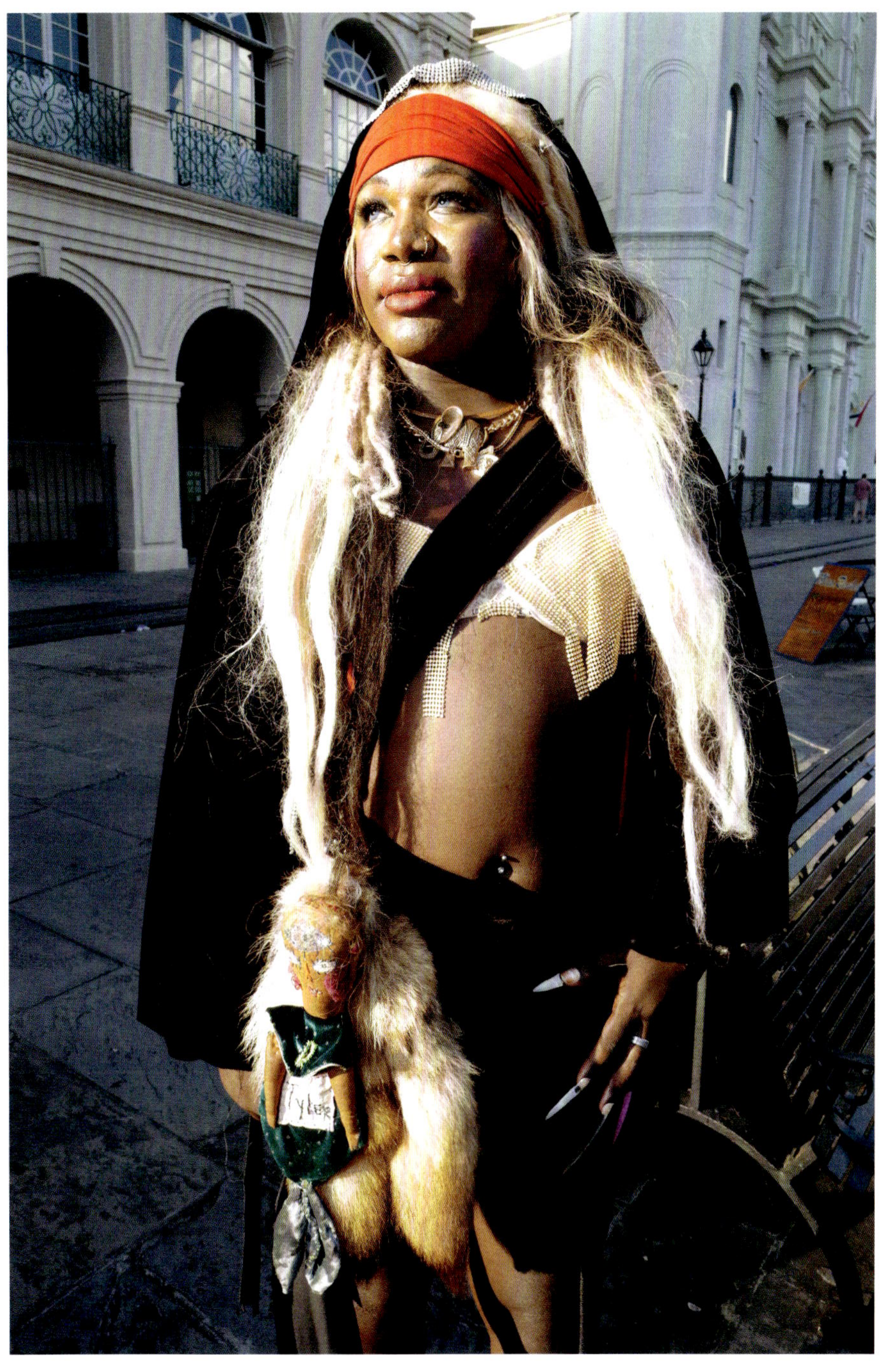

Tyler, Fortune Teller, New Orleans, Louisiana, 2021

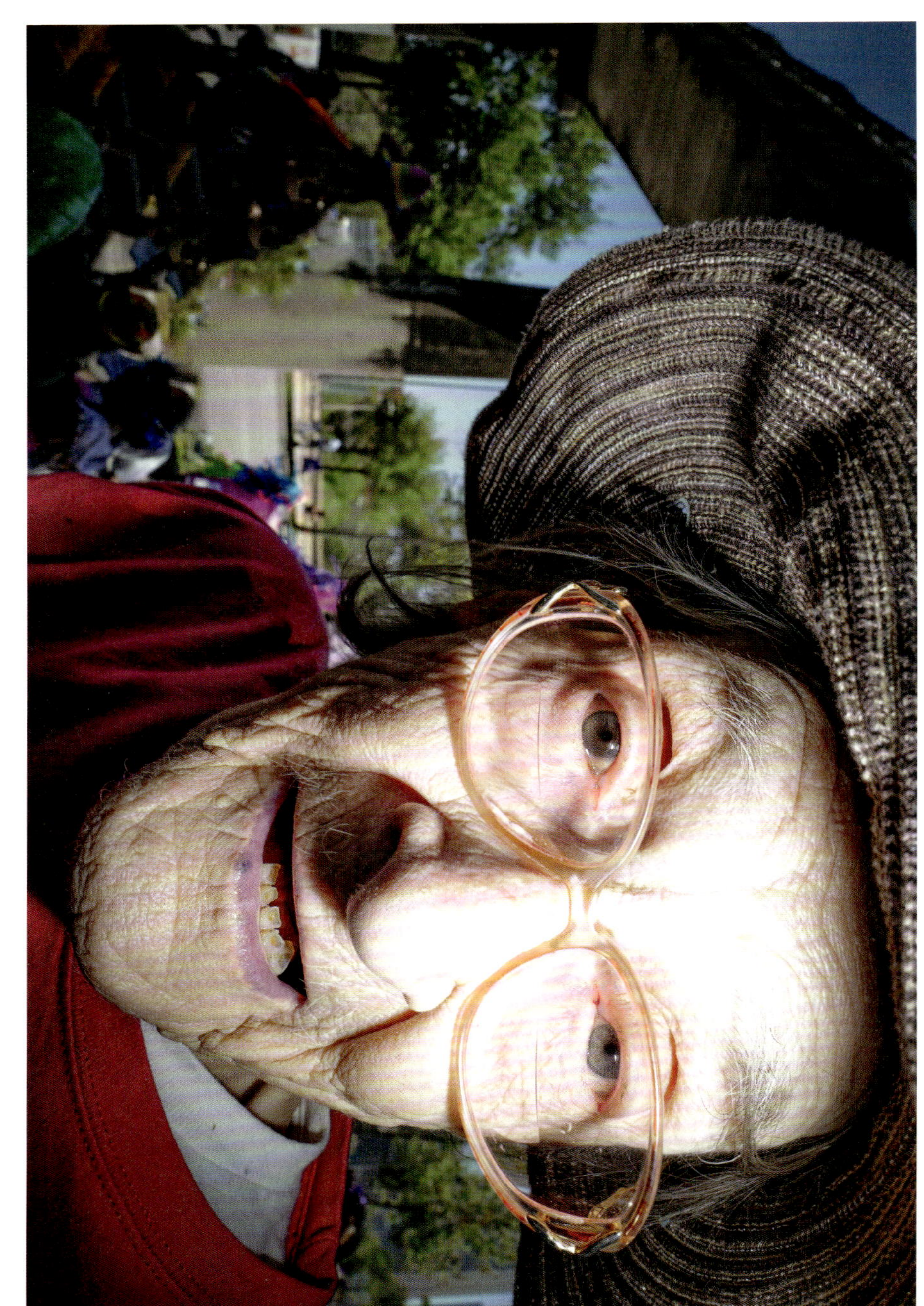

Donna, Veteran, Houston, Texas, 2022

Kat and Freddie traveled the whole of the United States "riding the rails." Every year, they returned to New Orleans to renew their marital vows. The year after I made this photograph, I saw Freddie without Kat. He told me that his "drunken rage had ended it all."

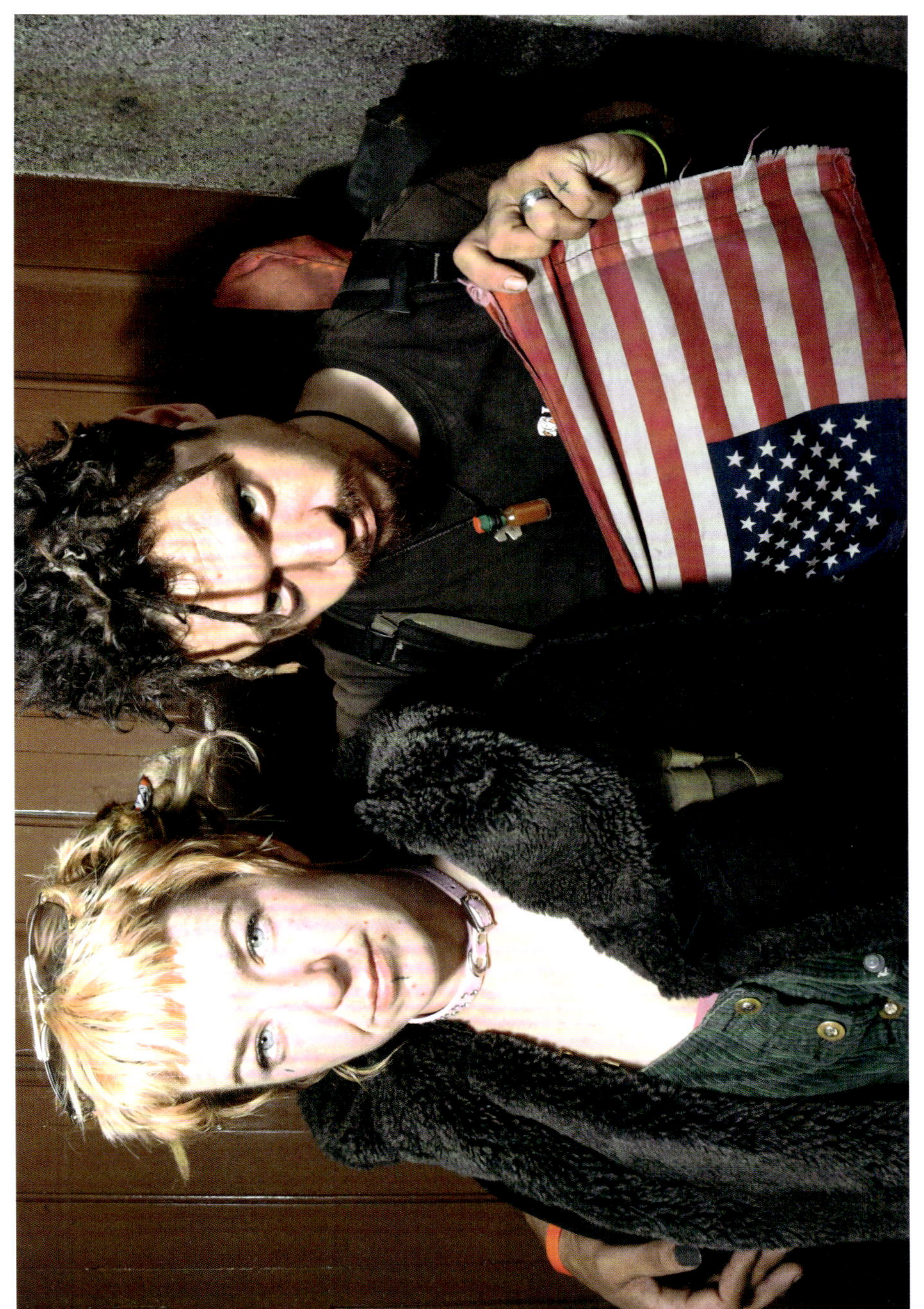

Kat and Freddie, Train Hoppers, New Orleans, Louisiana, 2018

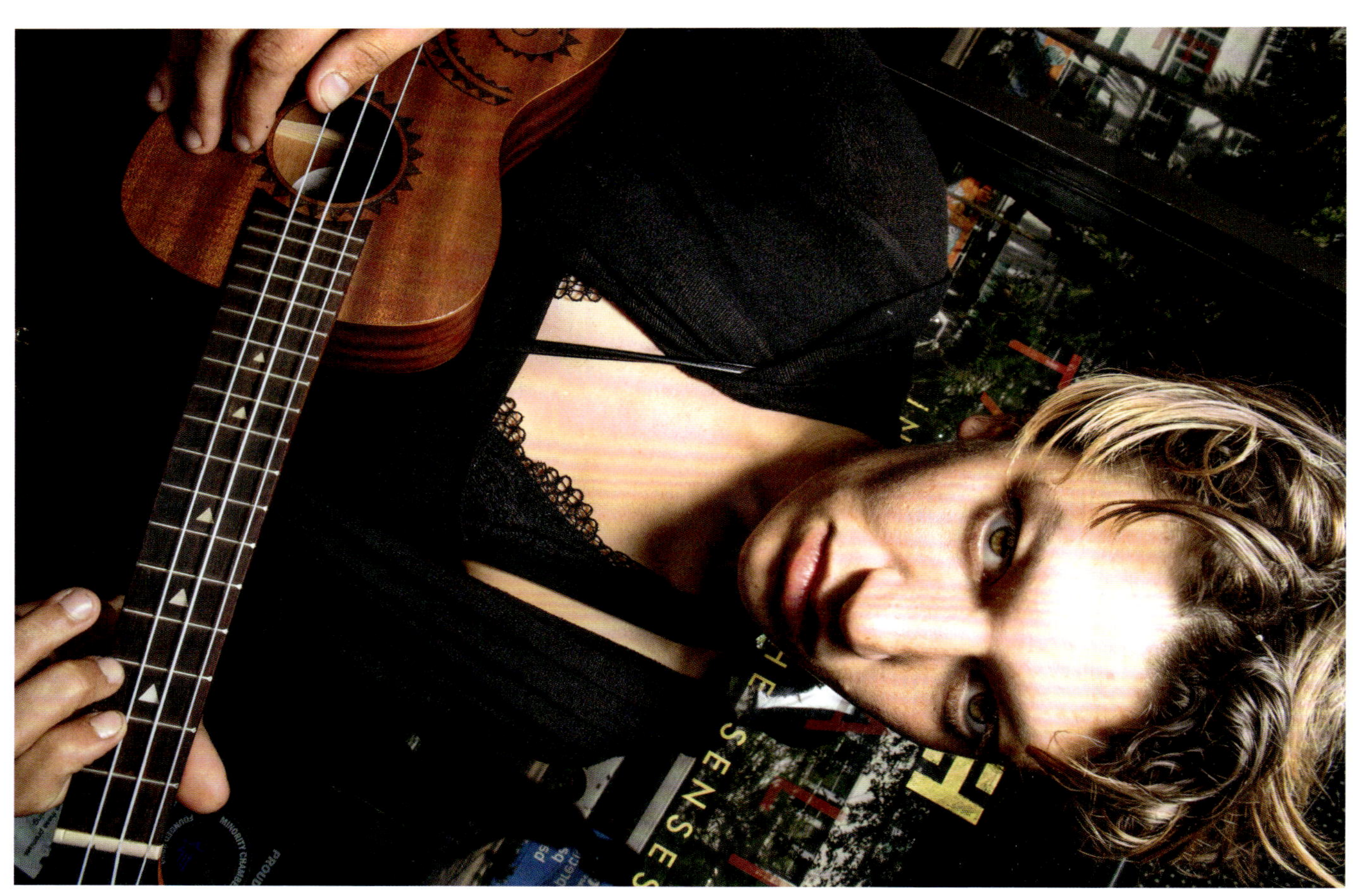

Bethany, South Beach, Miami, Florida, 2016

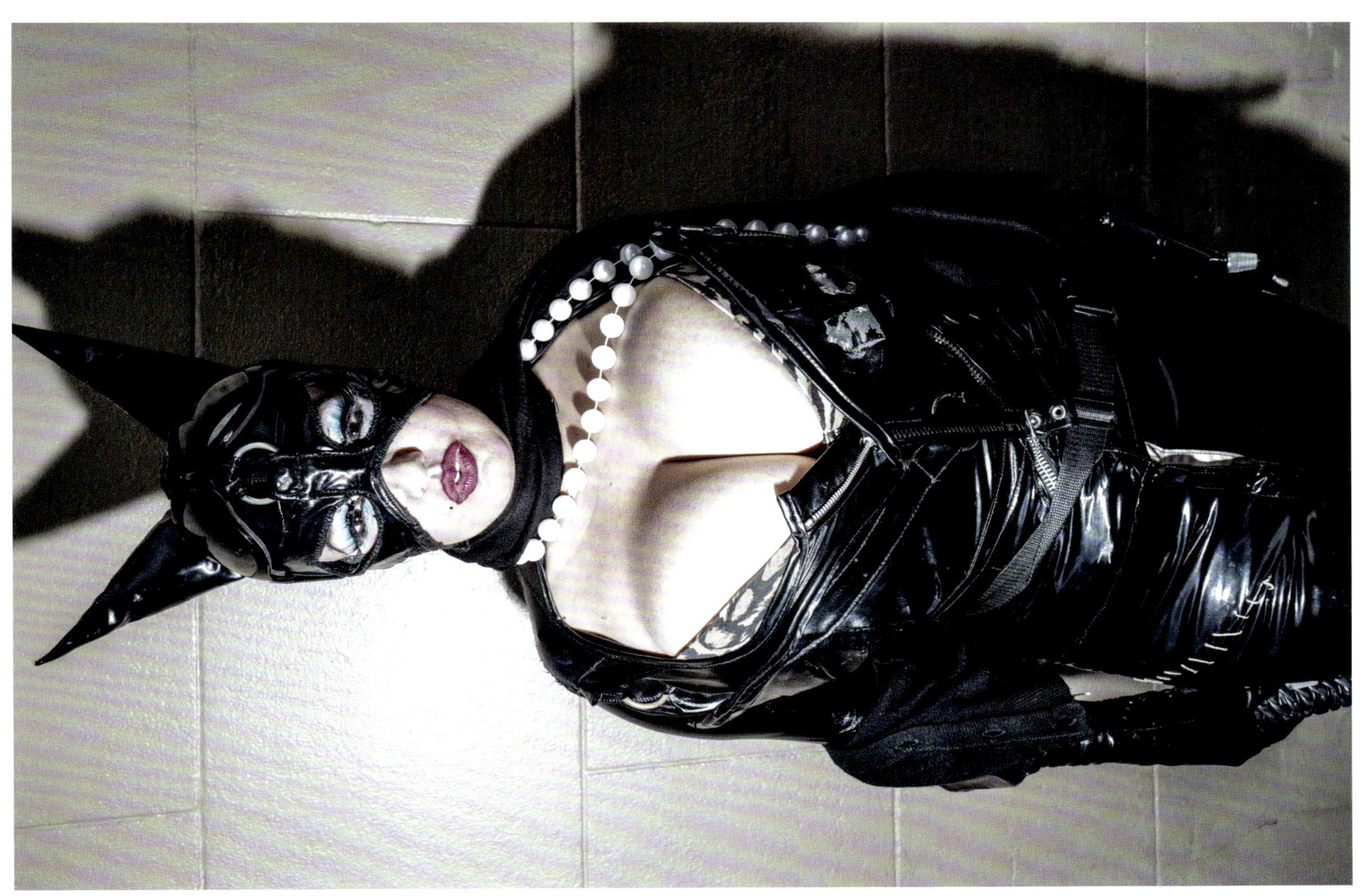

Loretta in Her Batwoman Outfit, New Orleans, Louisiana, 2020

"I know it's not a
real gun, but I like
the way it looks."

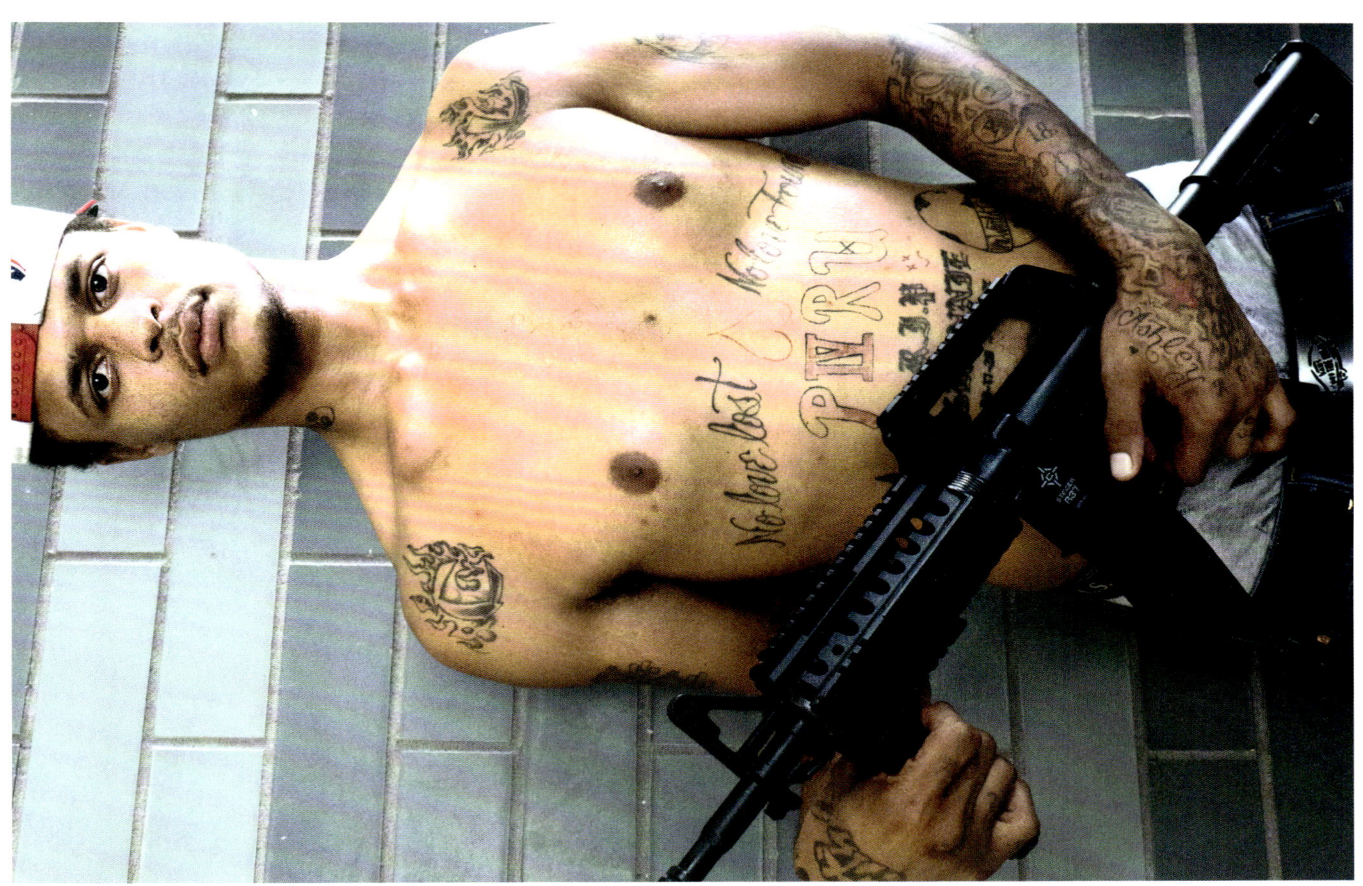

Ace with His BB Gun, Houston, Texas, 2016

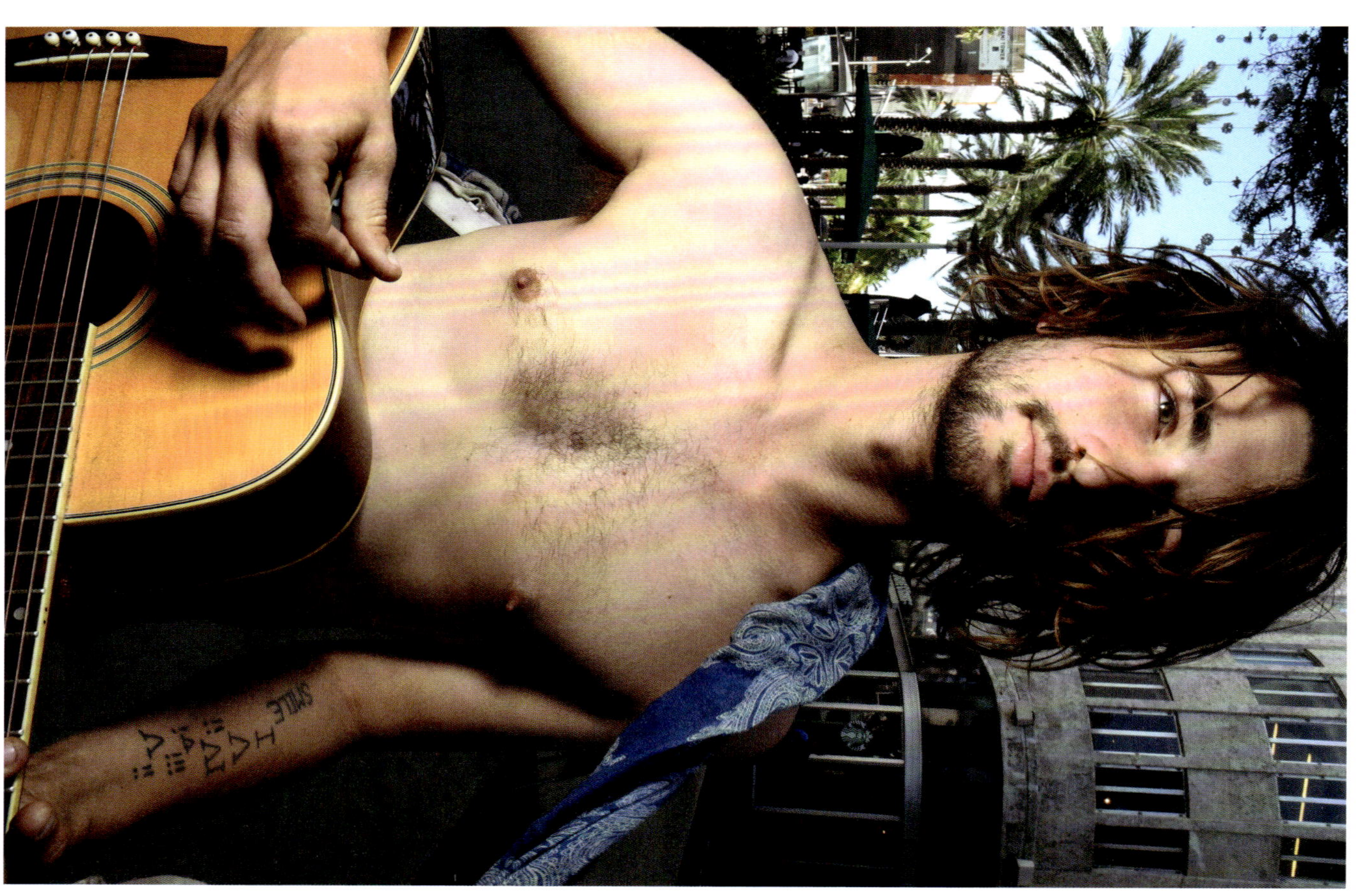

Justin, South Beach, Miami, Florida, 2016

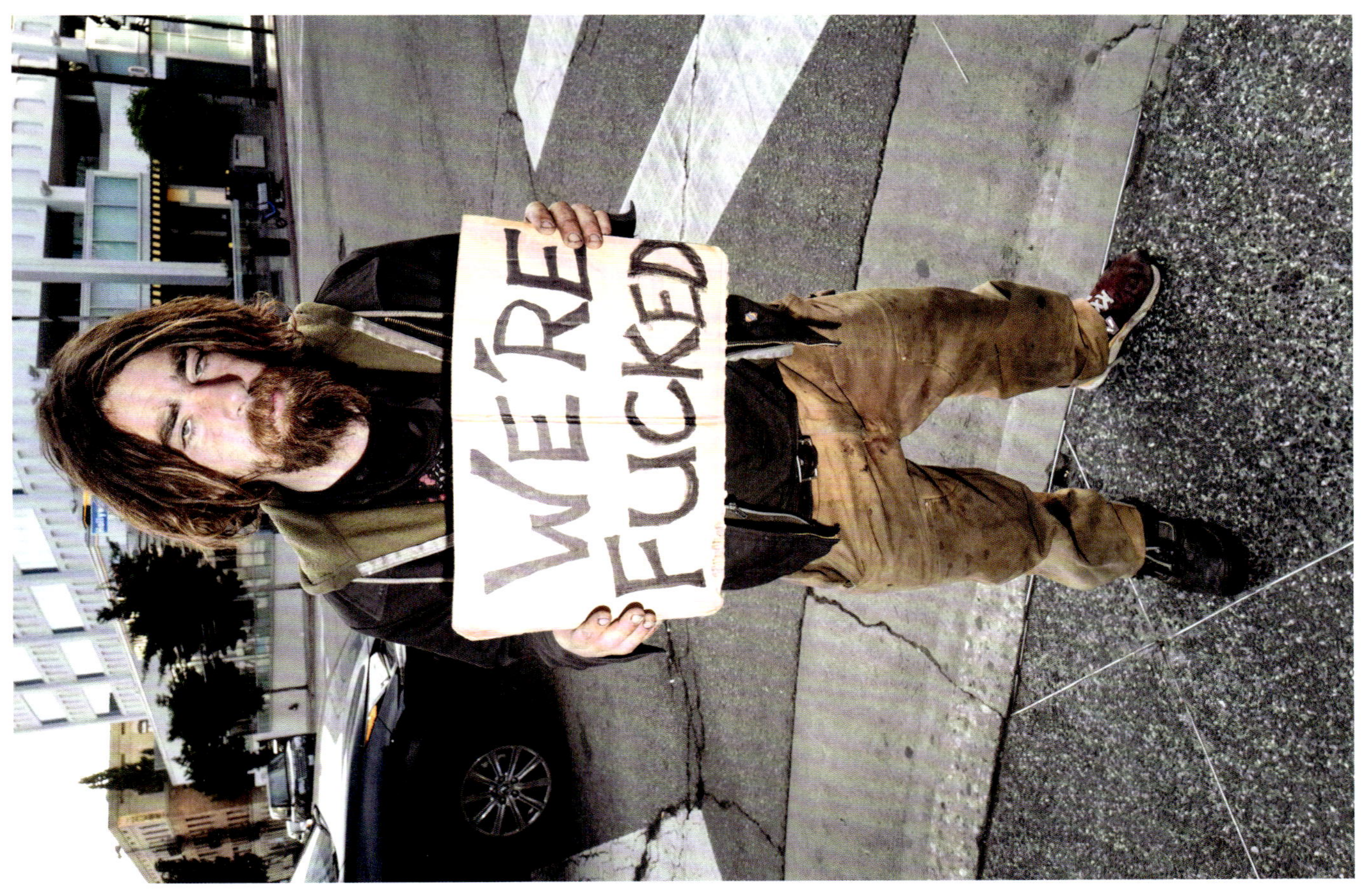

Man with Sign, Hollywood, California, 2020

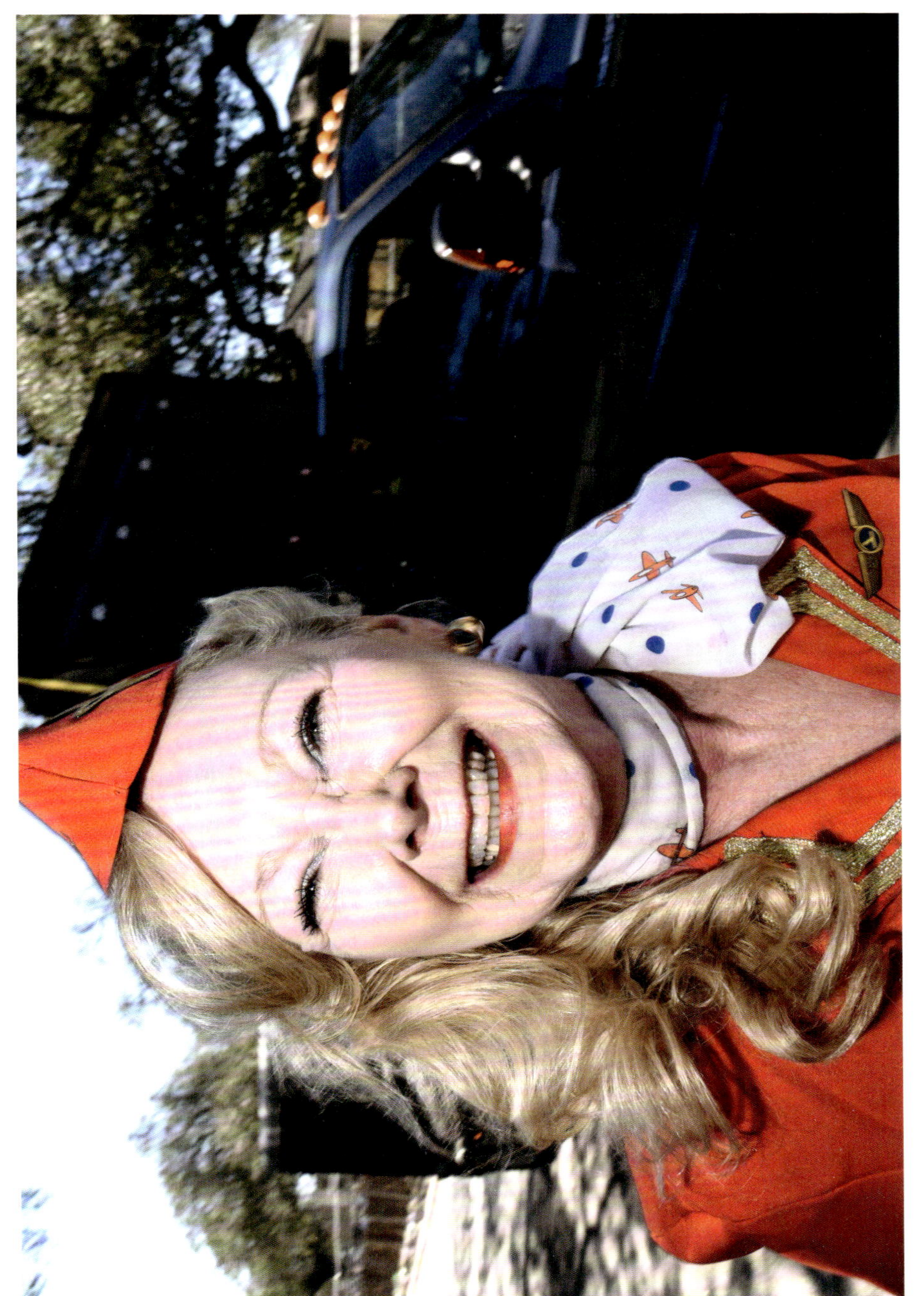

Flash-o-rama, New Orleans, Louisiana, 2016

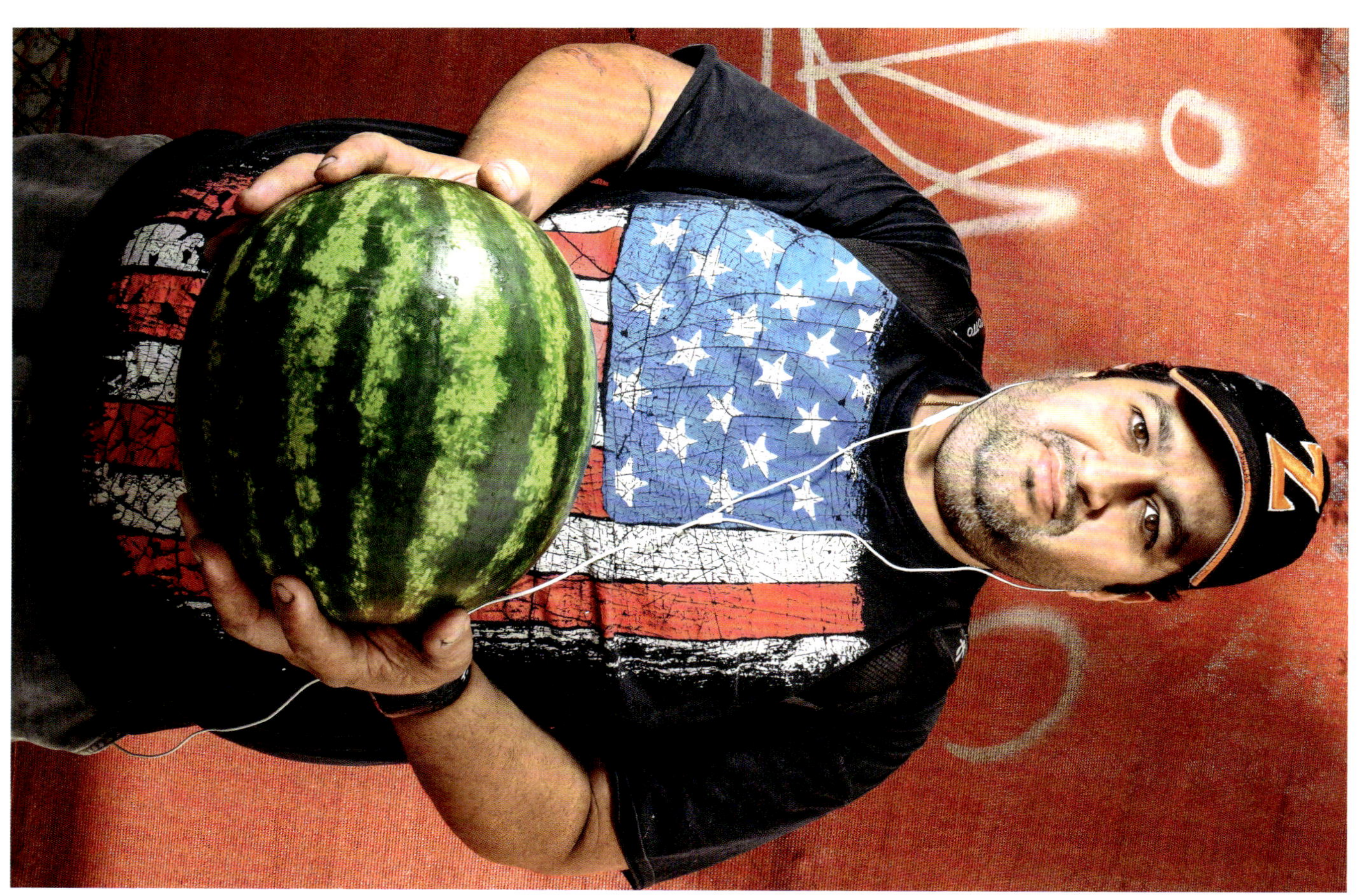

Man with Melon, Miami, Florida, 2017

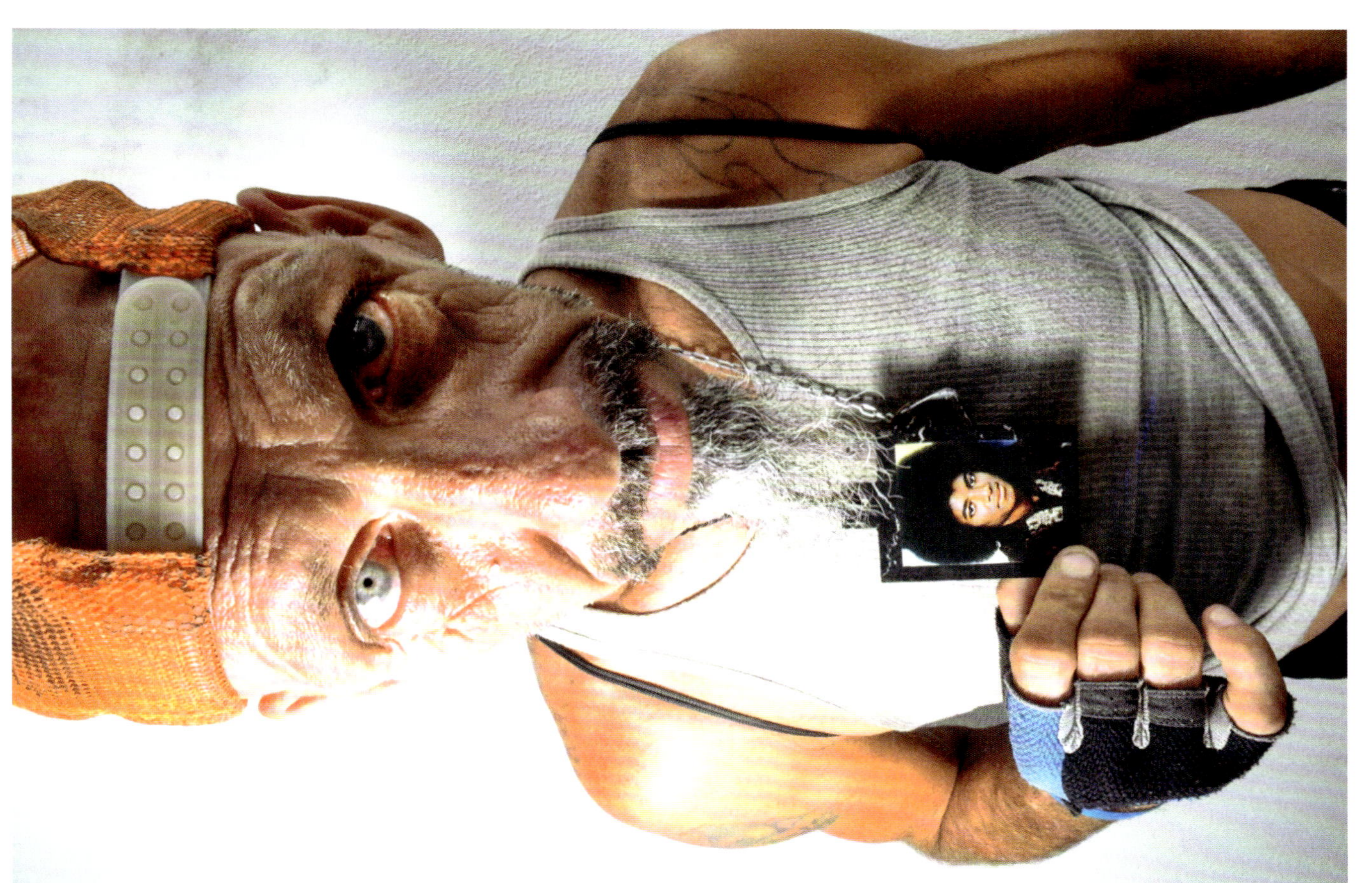

Kenny Showing His Guardian Angel, Miami, Florida, 2016

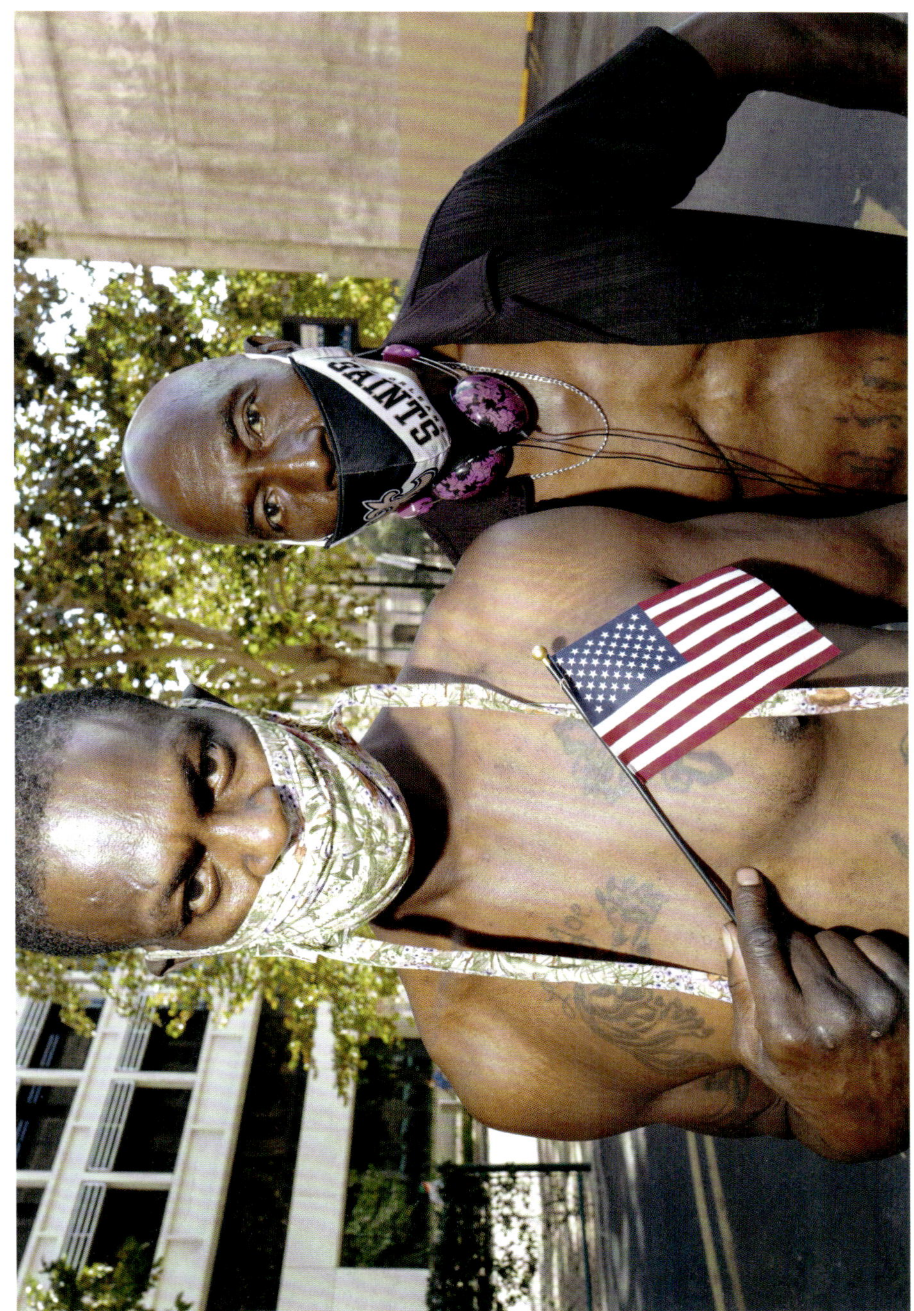

Election, Houston, Texas, 2020

Stephen and his
daughter were
homeless. She
went to live with
her mother and
gave Stephen her
backpack to help
him survive.

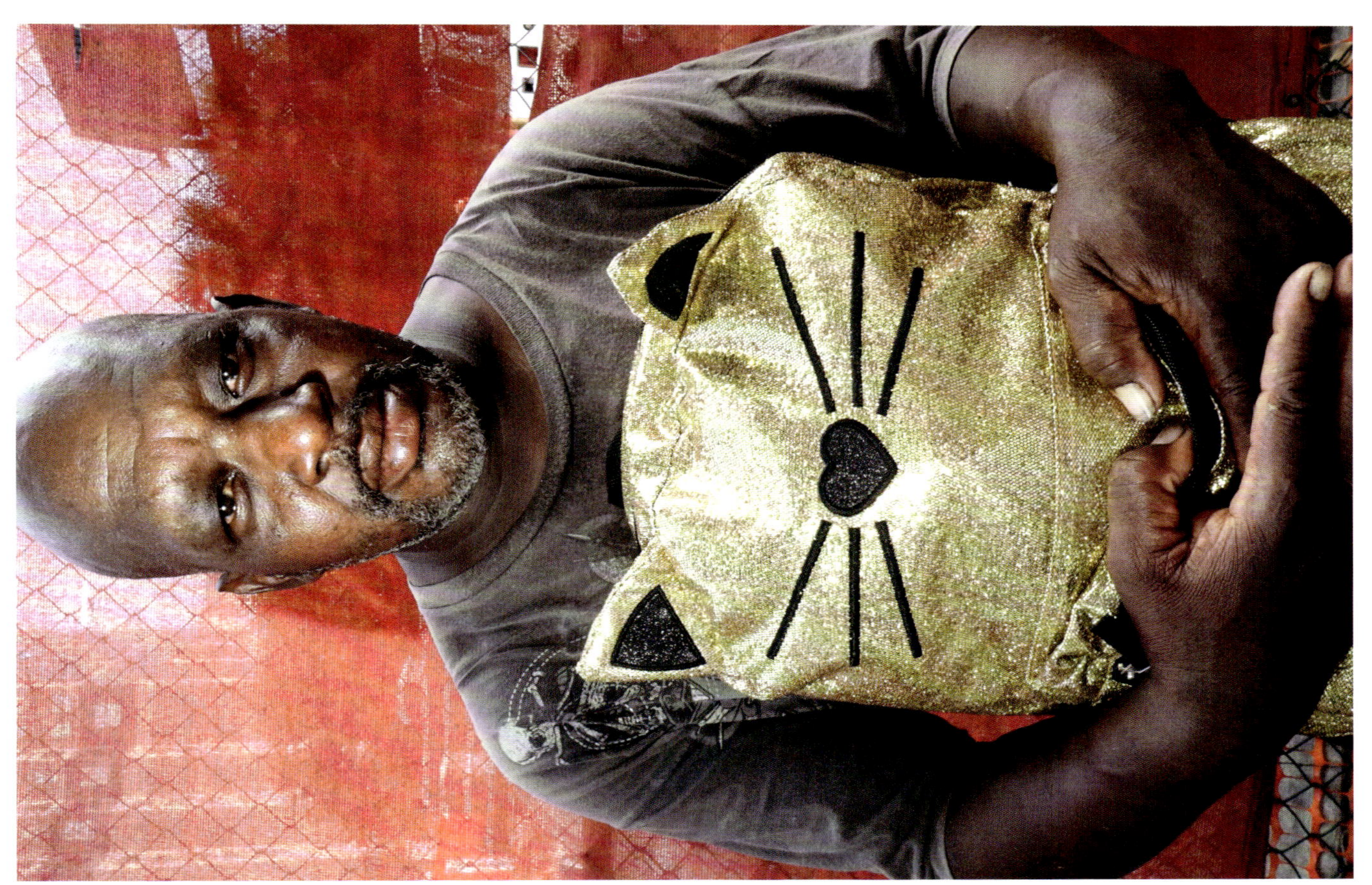

Stephen, Homeless, Miami, Florida, 2018

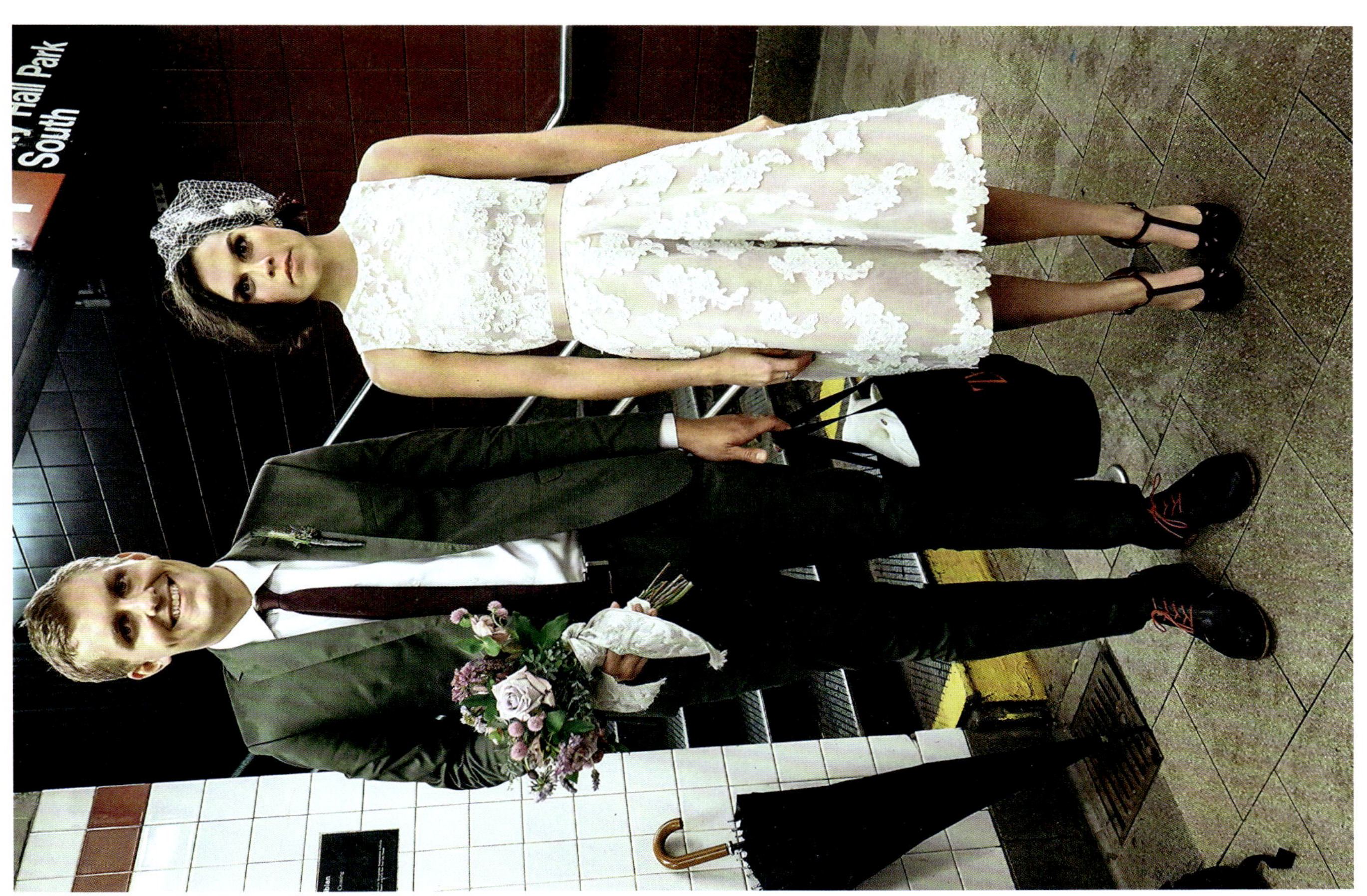

Couple in the New York City Subway, 2015

Two Women in NYC, 2015

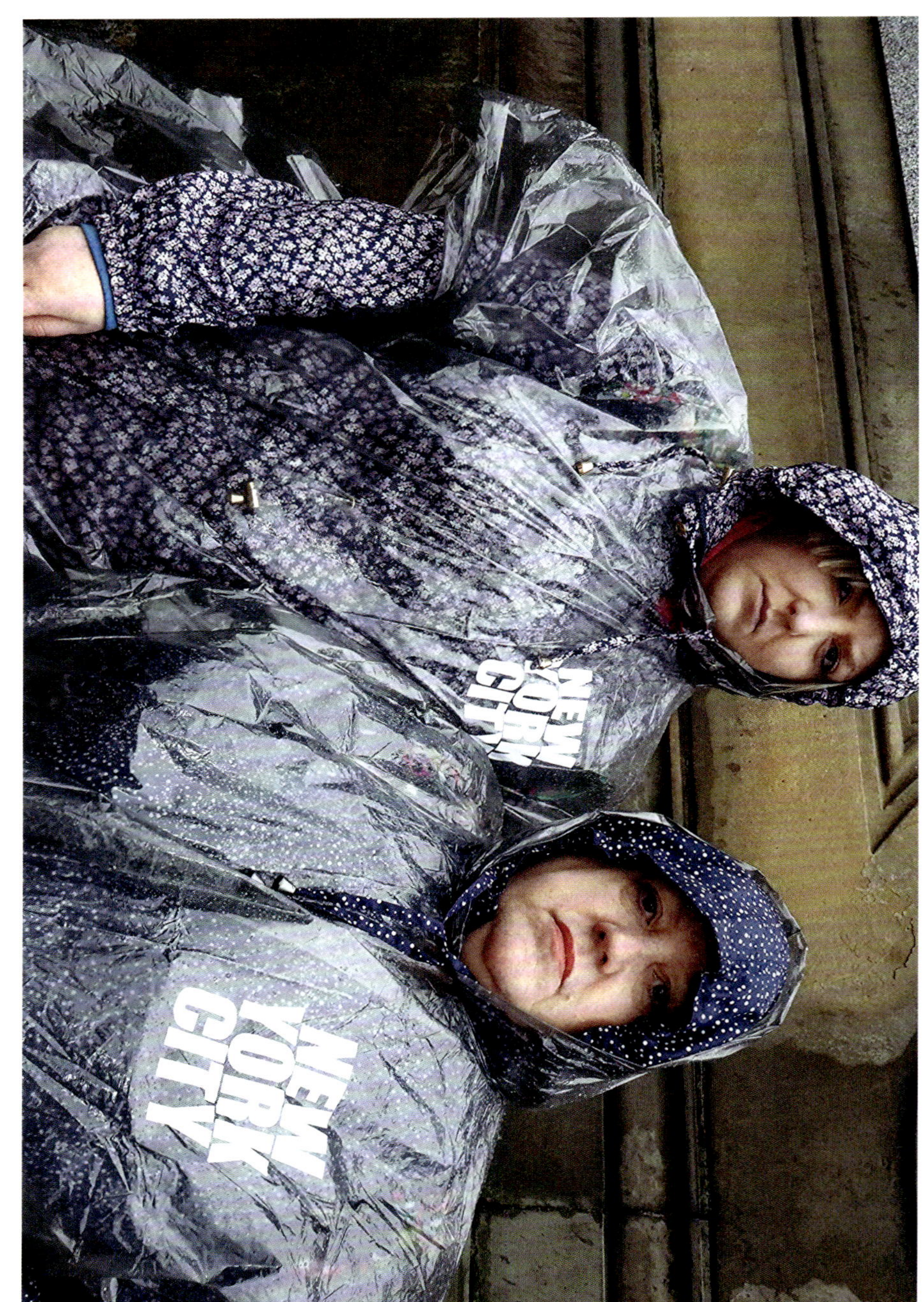

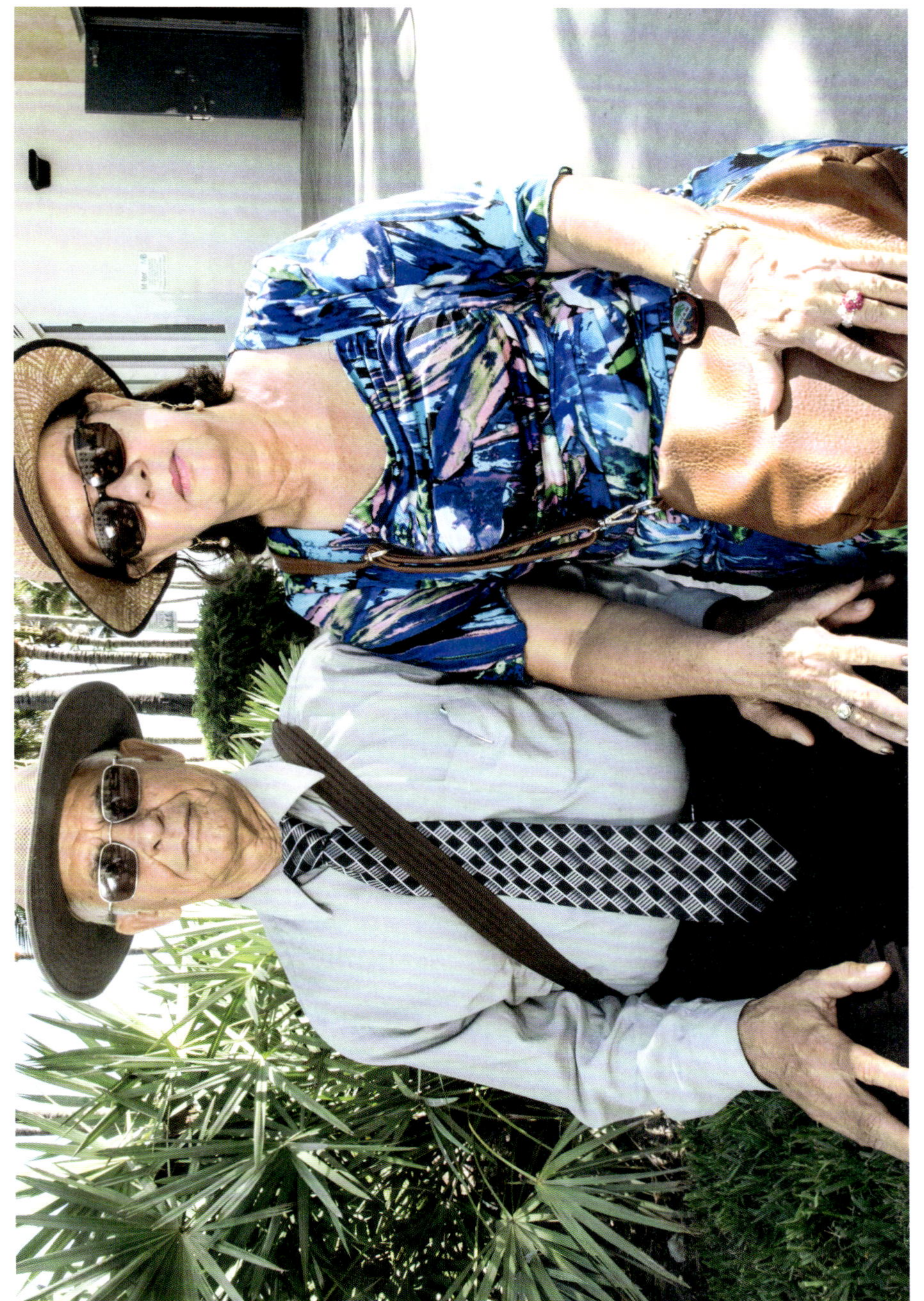

Tourists, Miami, Florida, 2017

I saw an
interesting
woman and
she gave me
permission to
photograph her.
I found out later
that she was
Jill Freedman,
a famous
NYC street
photographer.

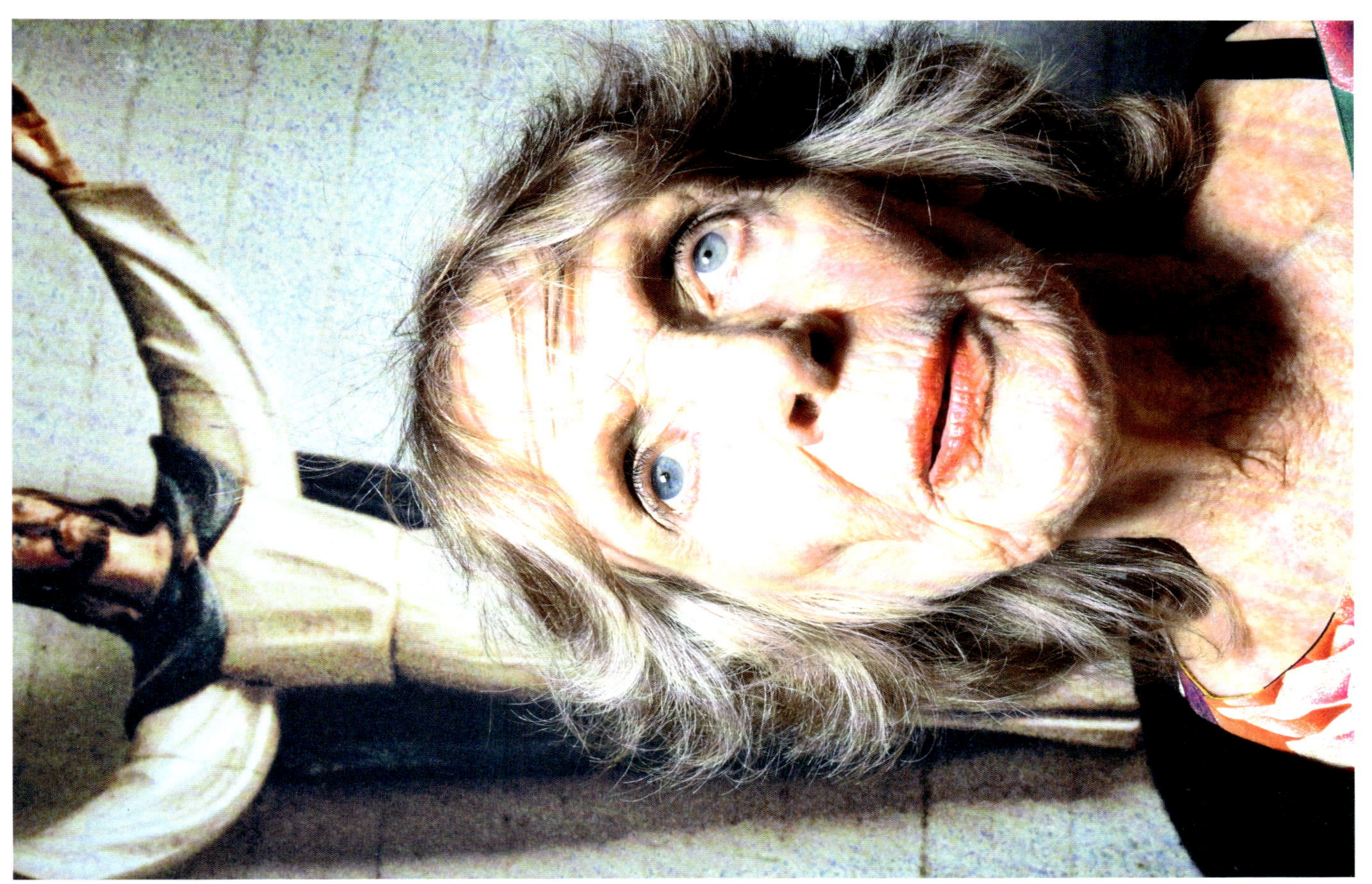

Jill, Street Photographer, Miami, Florida, 2016

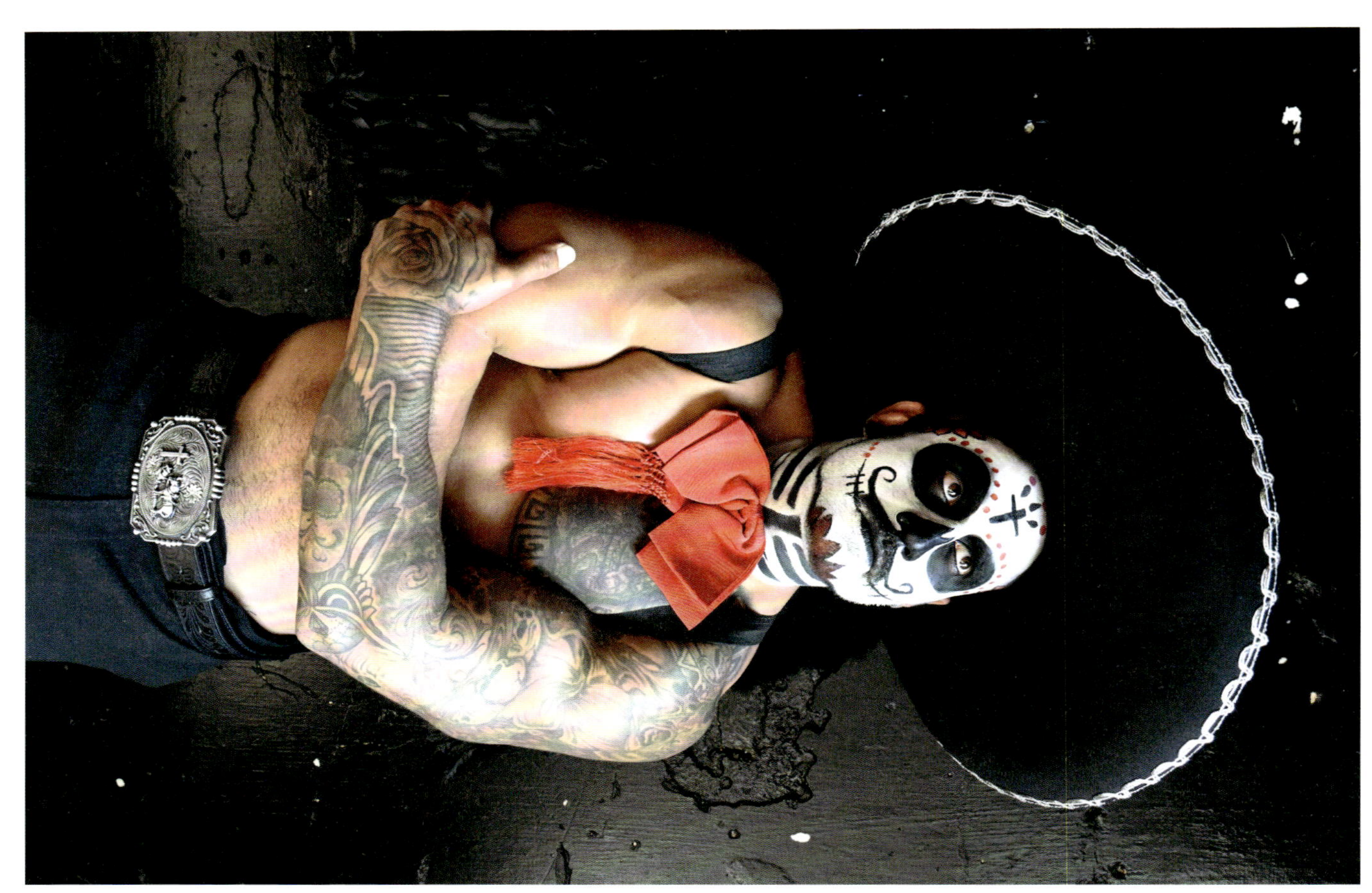

Gabriel at a Día de los Muertos Gathering, Houston, Texas, 2019

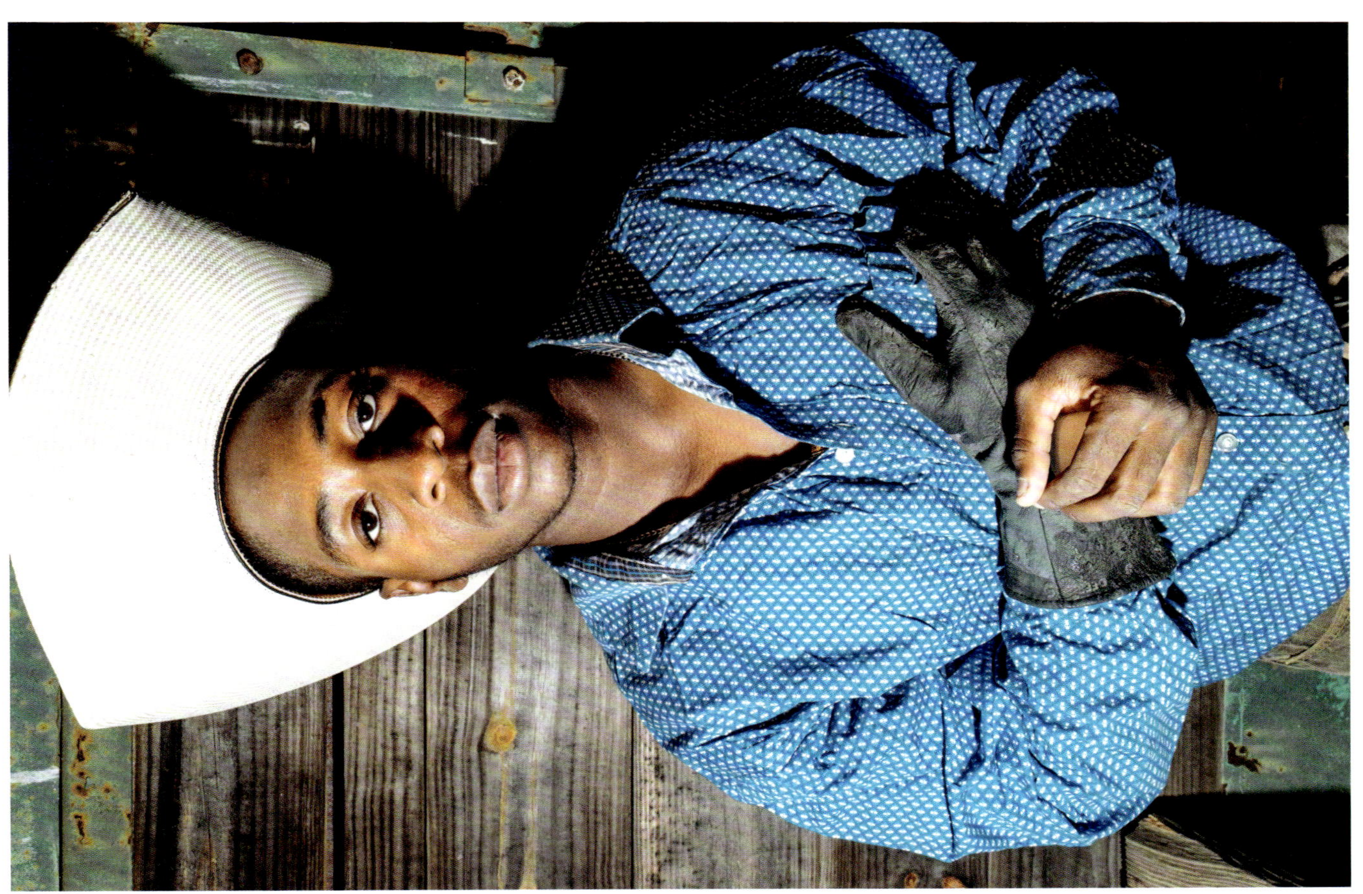

Ashton, Bullrider, New Braunfels, Texas, 2021

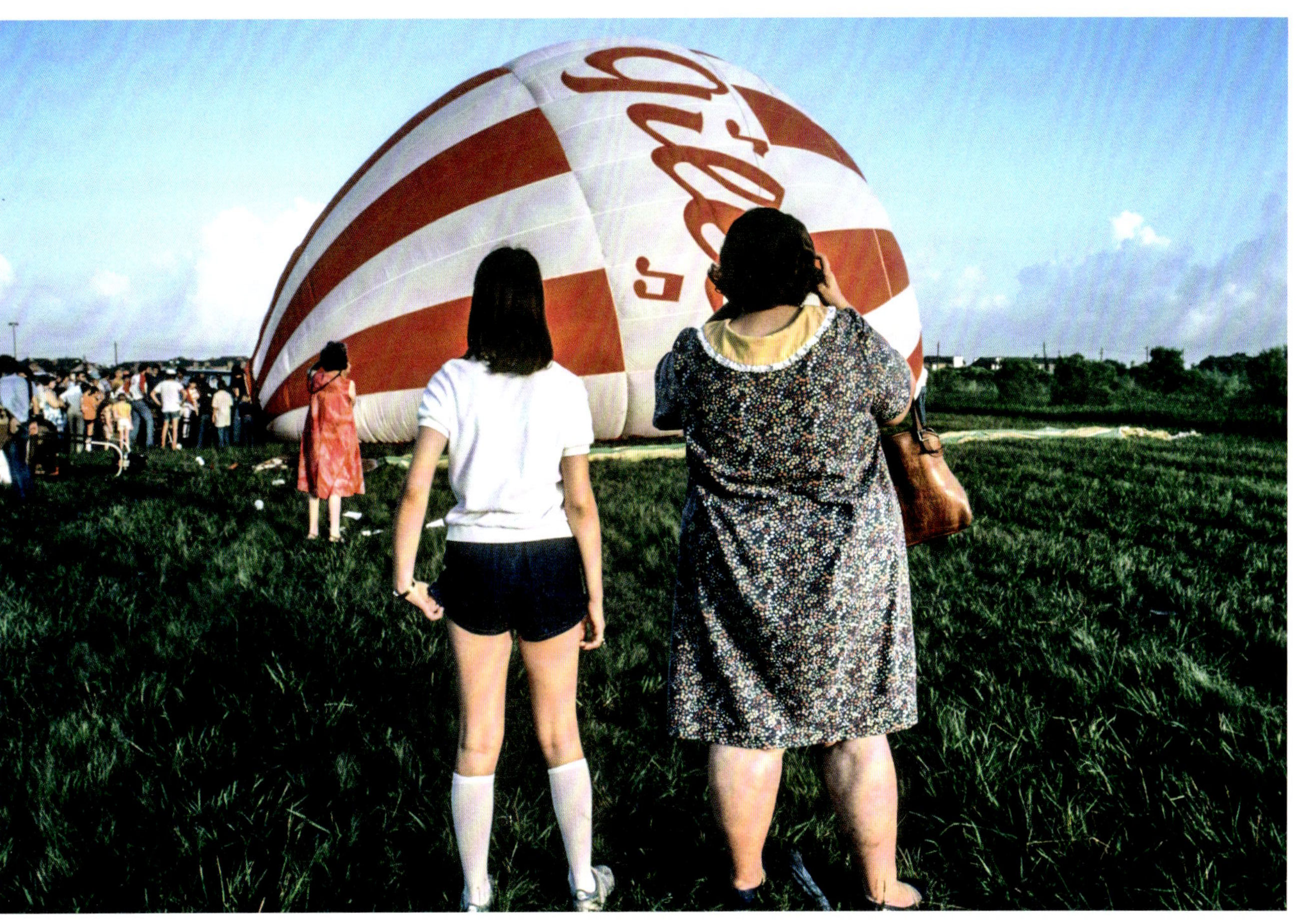

Balloon Day, Pasadena, Texas, 1975

INSIDE THE HEAD OF TOM "TBOW" BOWDEN

You may be interested in why I make photographs of people. It's a decades-long question I've asked myself. Here are some answers from a baggie full of scribbled notes that I keep by my bed.

It's my own form of therapy. Interesting people fascinate me. Making art is a critically important use of my time. Despondency and loneliness are common themes. My work is difficult, with an element of danger and fun. Stop being too careful. Learn to move quickly and be invisible. Existential answers are provided. Cameras are passports for seeking information and noisiness. Shine a light on the disenfranchised. Street photography is my religion and good exercise. Help others when possible. Provide a platform for dissent. Break the rules. Obey little. There's some time travel involved. Study light and time and space. Be on alert for hints of surrealism. Be here now. Look under the obvious. Practice social skills. Ask hard questions, do hard thinking. Ask, What happened? Why are we here, together? We are a wonderful spectacle, we are the human animal. Do it for the love of it all.

Wherever I go, whatever city I'm in, I head toward the streets. That's where the commotion is, that's where the people are, and that's where the images wait like presents. There is nothing more important to work on in my lifetime than this.

ACKNOWLEDGMENTS

I'd like to thank Maggie Steber for her thoughtful foreword to this book. Maggie is a well-known documentary photographer and a good friend.

I'd also like to thank Diane Arbus, Mary Ellen Mark, Richard Avedon, and Philip-Lorca diCorcia, who, through their work, showed me what compassionate street photography looks like.

And finally, thanks to Michael Itkoff at Daylight Books and the team of Ursula Damm and Gabi Fastman for their support and guidance.